"This guide for potential entrepreneurs explains how to get, evaluate, protect, develop and sell new products. . . ." Includes brainstorming techniques and exercises . . . market research, testing financial feasibility, patents, and trademarks. A lengthy 'resource guide' lists publications, associations, newsletters, small business development centers, government agencies and federal patent libraries, along with sample forms for confidentiality and licensing agreements."

—Publishers Weekly

"A book that's as entertaining as it is informative is a rare find. Husch and Foust pack in the valuable nuts-and-bolts advice, yet present it all in a breezy, fun-to-read style . . . A very thorough guide!"

—Information Marketing

"This *book* is a great idea. . . . Of special value are the chapters which discuss when to sell an idea or do it yourself, how to protect ideas, and how to present them for sale."

—National Home Business Report

"Well done. . . . Introduces novices and experienced inventors to the world of creativity. . . . Highly recommended as a text to be included in all libraries of serious or dilettante inventors."

—The Lightbulb
Inventors Workshop International Education Foundation

"Everything you've always wanted to know about developing your notion" is revealed in this "pithy new book." The authors "cover all the territory from conceiving ideas to signing royalty contracts. The strange thing is, they manage to entertain while they do it."

—The Daily Review

That's a Great Idea! "contains a great deal of facts and opinions that can benefit inventors. I recommend it as a reference book for both the neophite and pr‹

—Norman C. Parrish, President
Congress of Inventor Organizations

"This informative and entertaining volume is written in clear, easily understood language and includes an extensive resource guide.... *That's a Great Idea!* was written for anyone looking for the keys to getting and selling ideas."

—Technology Management News

"It's not easy to get a major company to look at your new idea, but this book gives you all the details on how it can be done with the best possible chance of success."

—Akron Business Reporter

"A step-by-step approach to idea development, from evaluating an initial concept to developing inspirations or new ideas, devising a promotion program, and applying for patents.... Contains an invaluable guide to government and business associations."

—The Bookwatch, Midwest Book Review

"Now there is a book you can read from cover to cover, or just dip into for the facts you need, that will fill the pitfalls for you. Many small manufacturers get their start with one product, but fail to grow because they are unable to follow up on their early successful act. This book just might be the catalyst that gets things moving."

—Agency Sales

"This books speaks to those who wonder, 'If I'm so creative, why ain't I rich?' After clearly defining what product and promotional ideas actually are, how to develop saleable ones, and how to expand one's perception of the marketplace and its trends, the authors readably provide the nuts and bolts of evaluating, refining, and choosing whether to manufacture or sell the idea.... Good advice abounds."

—The Idealog, Journal of the Brain Exchange

"A very useful guide.... Written by a successful entrepreneur and an attorney specializing in business law, it is a unique and stimulating handbook for new product success. Especially useful for potential entrepreneurs is the section on getting new product ideas."

—The Home Business Advocate

"Complete guide for generating, evaluating, developing, and protecting your ideas for new products and services. Includes brainstorming exercises and suggestions on how to select and approach potential sponsors. Also contains an informative resource guide and sample licensing and confidentiality forms."

—Marketing News
American Marketing Association

That's a Great Idea! "can help you channel your creative juices. The book constitutes a narrative checklist for both the creative and practical aspects of developing a new idea."

—The Newsletter on Newsletters

"Almost everyone has ideas for new products or services, but very few people know how to develop or sell them. *That's a Great Idea!* describes how it can be done. Readers of this book are assured of the best possible chance of profiting from a great idea.... *That's a Great Idea!* helps you know when and where to seek advice and assistance.... If you don't already have a great idea, the odds are extremely good that you will when you have finished reading the early chapters of this book."

—Selling Direct

THAT'S A GREAT

T   ANDBOOK

H

L   leas

↑☺
TEN SPEED PRESS
P O Box 7123
Berkeley, California 94707

Cover Design by Brenton Beck

Library of Congress Cataloging-in-Publication Data

Husch, Tony, 1943-
    That's a great idea.

      Reprint. Originally published: Oakland, Calif.:
Gravity Pub., c1986.
      Bibliography: p.213
      Includes index.
      1. New products. 2. Creative ability in business.
3. Inventions. 4. New business enterprises. I. Foust,
Linda, 1950-   . II. Title.
HD69.N4H87   1987   658.5'75   87-13891
ISBN 0-89815-218-6

Printed in the United States of America

1 2 3 4 5 — 91   90   89

CONTENTS

DISCLAIMER

This book is intended to provide information, entertainment, news value, and education on the subjects covered. It is sold with the understanding that the authors and publisher are not engaged in rendering legal or other professional advice. Professional services should be obtained if legal or other expert assistance is required.

The authors and publisher have made every attempt to make this book as accurate and complete as possible. The information included is believed to be reliable and to be based upon reliable sources. However, there may be mistakes of content or typography, and the authors and publisher make no guarantees, warranties, or representations of any kind. This book is designed as a general guide to the subject. The reader is urged to investigate and verify information and its applicability under any particular situation or circumstances.

The authors and publisher shall have no liability or responsibility to anyone with respect to contacts, negotiations, or agreements that may result from the information in this book, or for any loss or damage caused or alleged to have been caused directly or indirectly by such information.

ACKNOWLEDGEMENTS

Special thanks to all of the following for invaluable feedback and encouragement: Al Alcorn, Sally Alcorn, Dennis Baker, Claire Barnes, Rich Botto, Jane Byrd, John Foust, Sarah Fern Foust, Gil Friend, Bob Fuller, Rick Holderness, Ann Husch, Peter Husch, Jerry Mandel, Jim Reiter, Elizabeth Reynolds, Toby Schwartzburg, Kent Spence for the parking ticket lottery idea, Beverly Walsh, Benjamin Winter, Brandt Wolkin, and Sam Yiu.

THE AUTHORS

Tony Husch is a successful entrepreneur. While at Harvard College, he and two other students started the world's first computer dating service. He later established Husch Vineyards, one of the first small premium wineries in Northern California's Mendocino County. At the time, planting varietal grapes in this now-famous wine region was viewed as a crazy new idea. A recent new product success is his nationally distributed "Good Karmal" candy.

Linda Foust is a San Francisco attorney, world traveler, and poet. Her interest in the sources and limits of creativity and her practice of business law came together in her idea to write *That's a Great Idea! The New Product Handbook.*

CHAPTER 1: THE KEYS TO GETTING AND SELLING IDEAS

Did you ever see one of "your" ideas come onto the market—without you? Don't let it happen again. Most people have an idea for a new product or service, but no idea what to do with it. Why not take one of those million dollar notions out of your back pocket and turn it into a real product? Selling an idea to a company or developing a new product yourself can be challenging and rewarding. Bringing an idea or invention to market is a creative experience, perhaps the ultimate art form.

This book can be midwife for your brainchild. It will show you how to expand your generation of ideas and inspire more creative concepts than you ever thought possible. You will find out how to research and evaluate new product ideas and decide whether to sell a good one or develop and market it yourself.

That's a Great Idea! The New Product Handbook is a complete guide to getting new product concepts and evaluating, researching, protecting, perfecting, and presenting them for sale.

The next few pages introduce the keys to getting and selling ideas. They are the recurring themes of this book, and they apply at every step of the process. You will quickly learn how to use them. They are the keys to success in new product creation and development. Make a master set for your mind; use them to unlock your genius and open doors to new worlds.

- *You can control the creative process.* Are you waiting for a flash of inspiration or a stroke of genius to reveal the new product idea of the century? You needn't wait. It is easy to generate good, specific concepts on command. You can get and develop ideas at any time and operate at any level of expertise. This book contains the information that will show you how, including unique exercises to liberate and inspire the imagination. The entire series is a special training system for getting into condition to produce and develop great ideas. Try the exercises that suit you. Modify them. Invent new ones of your own. Consciously generating ideas creates the conditions for getting more of them.

- *An idea alone is not enough.* Undeveloped ideas are everywhere. They are difficult to protect and all but impossible to sell. Someone once said, "You only have to be smart for ten seconds." This is true if you are just talking about *getting* an idea. However, a concept must be *developed* in order to become a new product or service. You must demonstrate that it can be made and that people will buy it. This is true whether you intend to sell your idea to a company or produce it yourself.

- *Research, research, research.* Without good information, you are merely dreaming. Idea development requires constant research. You will seek out and study all kinds of data every step of the way. Your research should be like an intense treasure hunt you won't want to stop. Research to get ideas. Research to evaluate them. Research the market and the best pricing strategies. Research to find the right companies to approach. Research the market and pricing strategies. Research everything. The more you investigate and learn, the more excited you will get. You will "see" your product on the shelves long before it is actually "rolled out."

    The more you know about your concept, the better your chances are for selling it. Similarly, going into business and marketing your own product or service require extensive research and high-quality information. Many of the essential research aids are available in public libraries and from government agencies. Others are as close as the neighborhood shopping mall. Perhaps the most important research tools are the telephone and the Yellow Pages. *That's a Great Idea!* will serve as your guide to these and the various other tools of the new product trade.

- *Be ruthless in evaluating the viability of an idea.* Your favorite new product concepts will often be the ones you should discard first. "I like it!" or "It's so cute!" are not adequate reasons for risking your time and money. *The New Product Handbook* presents basic guidelines and special strategies for deciding whether to develop or abandon your ideas.

- *Decide objectively whether to sell an idea or produce it yourself.* Business is extremely competitive. It is essential to know your capabilities and limitations. The biggest decision you will make is how to develop your favorite brainchild. Will you sell your best concept or keep it to produce on your own? You will be able to make this decision after an honest evaluation of yourself and your great idea.

- *Be flexible and cover all angles.* Flexibility and thoroughness are necessary at all times. Keep an open mind for better ideas and consider all possibilities for how your product should look, feel, be produced and be marketed. Think of everything. Be ready to answer questions and make changes. If a company has a problem with the original concept, suggest another way of looking at it. Or restructure the concept slightly and present it to another firm.

  If you market something yourself, you need to monitor consumer response, reactions of competitors, new technology, and dozens of other matters. You must be ready to react quickly and effectively on all fronts.

Also maintain personal flexibility. You will be in a factory one day and a skyscraper the next. Interacting with many types of people in numerous economic and cultural environments may require dozens of different professional demeanors. You occasionally have to shuffle them so fast that you will feel like a quick-change artist.

- *Every new product or service is different.* This is not a step-by-step "how-to" book that presents *the* checklist for a typical new product. In fact, there is no "typical" new product or service, just as there is no "typical" company to which you will be presenting your ideas. Products range from short-lived, silly gimmicks to major technological breakthroughs. Companies are large and small, public and privately-owned, traditional and innovative. You decide how to apply the information and principles in this handbook. Your creation and development of a product concept from idea to roll-out, and beyond, is a unique story, and you are the author.

- *Newness alone is not enough: Successful new products and services must provide a consumer benefit, either real or perceived.* There are many ways something can be "new." Products may contain qualitative changes or unprecedented technical advances. Or "newness" may be simply a change of package, styling detail, or advertising slant. In any case, novelty alone will not guarantee success. Consumers must perceive a benefit for which they are willing to pay.

- *There are many ways to develop a concept.* If a truly great new product idea failed in one format, it may succeed brilliantly in some other form. Hang onto your treasured concepts and try everything before abandoning them.

- *You will spend your time or your money at every step.* You may do the development work yourself, or you can hire professionals. Base your trade-offs and choices on an honest and realistic assessment of your talents, available time, and financial capabilities. Know your limitations and always be willing to seek outside assistance to produce the best possible results.

- *Don't trust anyone, but . . . .* How do you protect yourself from imitators, con artists, idea pirates, business cycles, sunspots? How do you keep control of your new product concepts? Should you tell anyone about your idea? Who? How? When? Under what conditions? And how do you keep them from telling other people?

    In order to develop or sell ideas, you will have to disclose them. In fact, ideas get better when shared. Talk with people you trust to get feedback on your brainchildren and their proper upbringing. Share your ideas and adventures with family and friends so they will support you.

    Be discreet, but don't become obsessed with secrecy. There are no guaranteed protections anyway. Deal with reputable people, discuss your ideas only when necessary, and tell people when you expect a commitment of confidentiality. In most cases, you can rely on business ethics, common decency, and other modifications of the "Golden Rule."

- *Target your audience.* Although you should remain flexible, you must start with a well-defined analysis of who your "target" audience is and how to reach it. This refers not only to potential consumers of the product, but also to companies to which you will present your idea. Have good reasons for approaching each company you contact.

- *Be professional at all times.* Like it or not, business is influenced by image, and those people with a professional demeanor and presentation will inevitably command more attention and respect. Being professional includes everything from punctuality and appearance to making a complete and accurate product presentation. Although a financial outlay is sometimes be required to achieve the right result, professionalism is often simply a matter of attitude, good manners, and common sense.

- *Understand and use the profit motive.* Most business decisions are made upon an evaluation of how the bottom line will be affected. Do not make the mistake of thinking that a company will buy your new product concept simply because it is a great idea, or because you are convinced the world needs a portable electric potato peeler. Your primary task is to demonstrate the profit potential of your idea. Show that there is a demand for the product, that the concept is a logical addition to a company's current lines, that existing distribution systems are suitable, and so on.

- *Who you know makes a difference.* If your college roommate or your best friend in high school is now an Important Person at one of your targeted companies, it may help you get your foot in the door for a presentation. While not everyone will have such ideal connections, even the seemingly remote ones can be helpful. Somehow they establish a bond with the person you are approaching. The modern term is "networking." Utilize your contacts at every step. And start recording the names of people you meet. You may want to call them on your next project.

- *Investigate the appropriate legal protections.* Patents, trademarks, copyrights, and common law offer protections of different types to new product developers. Each may or may not be relevant for a

14

particular venture. There may be good reasons for not pursuing them in some cases. In theory, patents and trademarks protect and foster individual creativity. In practice, they often protect and favor big companies with money and skillful lawyers.

- *Follow the legal requirements for your product.* Someone going into business for himself will be concerned with the legal necessities for starting a company. There are also relevant considerations for selling a product or service idea to an existing firm. Federal and state governments have numerous laws affecting product development in many ways. Government agencies or an attorney can help you uncover and interpret the requirements.

- *Be honest with yourself.* Self-awareness is important. What are your motivations? Are you after money? Fame? Power? Something else? Whatever your real objectives and hidden intentions are, the more you recognize and accept them, the more your venture will succeed. If you believe in what you are doing, you will be happier. And so will everyone with whom you deal.

- *You will make mistakes; learn from them.* Mistakes are inevitable. There are no crystal balls in the new products business. With luck, your mistakes will not be too costly. Those that hurt the most often provide valuable insights and wisdom.

- *Act now.* If you want to try to sell an idea or develop a new product or service on your own, do it! Don't procrastinate. Don't put off starting, and don't stop half-way. You will find new, educational, and fascinating experiences at every step.

- *Persevere.* Companies do not actively solicit outside ideas for new products. It will not always be easy to reach them. Most large firms have their own new product or research and development departments that know the needs of the company much better than you do. If you don't get a positive response from a firm the first time, consider the experience good practice and keep trying. Perseverence is also essential for success in starting a business with a new product idea.

Summary

These themes occur again and again in the process of getting and selling ideas. Learn them. Use them. They are your keys to success.

That's a Great Idea! is primarily about creating, designing, and marketing new consumer products and services, but the principles apply to developing any good concept. It may be anything from a silly gismo to a plan for a real estate development or a premise for a blockbuster movie. The soul of this book is its inquiry into the nature and practice of idea generation, evaluation, and implementation.

As you read *The New Product Handbook*, you will notice that it is sometimes fanciful, sometimes straightforward and down-to-earth. In that respect it mirrors the nature of new product creation and development. You must get used to listening to the zany voice of your wild side *and* to the sober voice of your thoughtful side. You will master not only the realm of unbridled imagination, but also the more methodical, serious aspects of making ideas real by bringing them to life as new products.

CHAPTER 2: GETTING NEW PRODUCT IDEAS

The *GoochyGoo* *Chronicles*

Damn! Damn! DAMN!! Why am I fixing this kitchen sink on a beautiful Saturday afternoon? I'd rather be sailing. Or playing tennis. Or thinking of other things I'd rather be doing . . . . . At last, almost done. Just reconnect everything. Oh no, where's the pipe goop? If I put these pipes back together without it, they'll never come apart again. What else could I use? Oh yeah, Vaseline. It's not as messy as that smelly plumber's goop, and probably better . . . . . Damn! I can't find any Vaseline either. None in the bathroom, none in baby's room, none in the shop, none here in the car. I may as well drive over to the mall and buy a jar . . . . . Here it is. Gosh, a new tube. I'll just pick up a couple of these little babies to put around the house. Mercy! Look at that price! That's new, too. A buck seventy-nine for an ounce of petrolatum. That's insane! I'm going to get a cheaper brand . . . . . Nothing. I've looked all over the store. There are no other brands of petroleum jelly. I'm going to the hardware store for the smelly goop . . . . . Hey! Wait a second. If there are no other brands, that means there is no competition for Vaseline. That's incredible! Everything else has lots of competition, but there's only one petrolatum. This could be a golden opportunity . . . . . ♩♫♪ Thank heaven for little tubes . . . . . ♩♪♪

Almost everyone has a great idea for a new product. You probably do, too. People usually keep these concepts stashed away in the backs of their minds. They think such ideas will be stolen or perceived as silly and unworkable, so these new product notions often go unshared. But if an idea is not shared or developed, it may "get away." Someone else may get it and develop it.

Do you ever wonder how some people keep coming up with new ideas? These individuals are continually creative and, frequently, a little silly. They work on and share their notions. Their ceaseless flow of ideas indicates that consciously getting and developing concepts create the right conditions for the generation of new and better ones.

Although some people just naturally seem to have an unlimited supply of ideas, getting them is a skill that anyone can master through receptiveness, awareness, and practice. You can *create* ideas, without waiting for a stroke of genius. You do not need any special talents or expertise. Throughout history there have been individuals who produced theories and inventions in widely varied fields without formal training. In fact, lack of a technical background can be beneficial because there are fewer disciplinary traditions and supposed technological limitations to constrain the imagination. The most important factor seems to be the creative frame of mind.

The first three chapters of *That's a Great Idea !* present extensive checklists and unique exercises to put you in the right frame of mind for getting and playing with a great many new concepts. But, first, it is helpful to explore the nature of that frame of mind.

The Two-Sided Brain and the Two-Stage Process of Getting Ideas

There has been much research into the nature of creativity. A relatively recent focus for this interest has been the discovery of the brain's bilateral structure. The human brain is divided into two hemispheres, each of which perceives reality differently. One side of the brain is always dominant. In most people it is the left.

The left side of the brain is the one cultivated in school. It controls language, logic, counting, and classifying capabilities. It is verbal, analytical, objective, sequential, and orderly. It processes information one segment at a time. The left judges, censors, criticizes, edits, and revises.

The right brain is the intuitive, illogical side. It is creative, imaginative, and prone to sudden insights and associations. It utilizes symbolism and instantly recognizes patterns among seeming chaos. The right side does not keep track of time and is not able to classify things. It is spontaneous and subjective. It comprehends complicated wholes in a flash.

The right side of the brain is capable of generating numerous ideas and breaking us out of normal ways of seeing the world. But, due to the greater emphasis placed on left-brain activities in education and most employment situations, the right hemisphere is usually underdeveloped. In order to use it, we sometimes have to trick the left side into shutting down by giving it a nonrational task. Rather than struggling, the left side will give up and allow the creativity of the right brain to take over.

Getting new product ideas is a two-stage process. First, you stimulate your right brain to generate as many concepts as possible, no matter how crazy or silly or embarrassing they may seem. In stage two, you let your analytical left brain judge and refine. Your rational side will edit and evaluate, and it may also see modifications to make wild ideas workable.

The role of the logical left brain in stage two is as important as that of the right brain in the first stage. We will return to the left side in Chapter 5, *Evaluating Ideas*. Meanwhile, these initial chapters will focus on how to utilize your right side for generating ideas. Here are a few suggestions and proven guidelines for the process:

- **Suspend judgment.** This is crucial. Do not judge or analyze anything, as this lets the left brain take over again. Ignore logical constraints and technical impossibilities. Consider yourself nothing more than a receptor for ideas which have been sent out into the world from whatever mysterious sources. The time for evaluation is later.

You are interested in quantity, not quality. More *and* better ideas are generated by deferring criticism and analysis. Once you have an idea, build on it. Modify it. Think of variations. Your goal in this first phase is to create an avalanche of concepts.

You may be as wild and uncensored as you want. People in corporate new products departments "brainstorm" in groups. Because the threat of embarrassment could be inhibiting, they strive for an open, nonjudgmental environment. You should do the same.

Give yourself permission to be uninhibited. Some of your craziest ideas will turn out to be your best, either in their original form or as modified by later refinement. And the emphasis here is on "later." Where would the sewing machine be today if the idea for putting the eye in the *point* of the needle had been rejected out of hand as outlandish?

• *Write down your ideas.* Sometimes great notions come unexpectedly, and it is amazing how quickly even the most "unforgettable" ideas can vanish. Then it's like trying to remember a dream that remains just out of reach. Recording your concepts frees you from having to remember them. This maintains space in your mind for new ones to enter.

Ideas sometimes seem to have lives of their own. If you don't take one in, it will continue traveling around until it finds another person who will preserve and develop it. There are innumerable stories of "synchronicity," in which one individual's concept suddenly turned up as someone else's new product. It seems that ideas do have their "times" and that if *you* aren't willing to act on one whose time has come, it will seek out someone who *is*.

Immediately recording your concepts also maintains your creative frame of mind. It keeps you from getting side-tracked into thinking an idea through in detail. The time for that is later. Have pen and paper or a tape recorder with you at all times. Small notebooks and miniature pencils will fit in any pocket or purse. Keep all your notes. Months, or even years, later you may find a use for an idea that had no special significance at the time you wrote it down.

- *Practice.* As in athletics, training and conditioning do improve performance. Stretch yourself to the limits in each creative session. One roadblock to getting really good ideas is simply stopping too soon. Instead of searching for the one best solution, look for the *most* ways of solving a problem. Set quotas for the number of ideas you must get. When you reach your quota, think of five more.

- *Observe.* Learn how to get into a creative frame of mind at other times. Develop the habit of *noticing* existing products and ways of doing things. Observe and wonder what would happen if conditions or methods were changed. Try to *see* things as if they were unfamiliar, as if you were a visitor from a foreign country. These techniques will help you break the barriers of familiarity and habit.

- *Go to a new locale.* Different surroundings can take you out of your usual patterns of thinking and pave the way to new insights.

- *Expose yourself to plenty of input.* Sensory and intellectual input provides the seeds from which ideas sprout in the imagination. The richer the preparation, the more concepts and associations will come up. Be aware of current trends. Sometimes it is effective to let your mind loose in a specific category, such as communication, transportation, food, clothing, health, building, energy, basic materials, tools, and so on. Other times it is most effective to let your mind roam among these realms and create linkages. Some of the most successful new products arise from the overlapping of ideas or solutions to problems in more than one area.

21

- *Make originality a goal.* We usually perform better when we have standards to meet. Know in the back of your mind that you are striving for original concepts, great new ideas.

- *Use the remedies for getting "unstuck."* There are certain techniques to use when you feel you are getting nowhere. Get out of the world of thoughts and into the world of things. Doodle with pen and paper. Build something out of blocks. Cut out pictures and paste them together. Handling real things can cause the glimmer of an idea that will get you going again.

  Another method is to shift your emphasis. Reformulate the question. Think of an analogous problem and see how it was solved. For example, look to nature. How have plants or animals solved questions of transportation or cooling or camouflage?

  Try association games. Select two seemingly unrelated words and force an association between them. Choose two completely unrelated objects and find something they have in common. Pick a word at random from the dictionary and force a connection, no matter how strained, with the topic you are considering. This will start a train of thought or produce an insight.

  If you are working on the solution to a particular problem, try to think of ways of cheating. By refusing to observe established rules, you will break out of patterns of thinking that may be inhibiting creativity.

- *Let your ideas incubate.* Concepts may not come immediately, but will sometimes surface unexpectedly after your brainstorming sessions. Many great innovations of the past came to their creators while they were engaged in mundane activities. Occasionally, it is wise to leave a problem for a while. The solution will often be there when you return.

• *Start now.* Getting started is not always easy. There are other demands on your limited time. Reserve a certain period for creative thinking. Make a date with yourself and keep it. Decide on a realistic schedule, and then consider it inviolate. You need not sit at a desk to have ideas. Use your exercise time, commute, or household chores as your creative period.

Utilize the following checklists and exercises to get yourself going. Or simply choose a topic and begin. Sometimes it is effective to brainstorm with a friend, but only if you agree to suspend judgment and evaluation until later. Start thinking quickly of names, needs, changes, functions, devices. Let your thoughts and associations flow freely. Extend each thought. Vary it. Turn it upside down. Take it to an extreme. The further out you go, the better. Dream up advertising slogans and packaging concepts. See if those ideas suggest others. Write down everything.

You might even consider setting up an "idea studio." Find a space you can call your own. Select several items from the checklists and write one each on blank sheets of paper. Tack these to the wall and brainstorm them all at once. Write your ideas for each topic on its sheet. You may want to use different colored pens or markers. Concepts from one category may stimulate ideas in others. There are no limitations.

Checklist for Creating New Product Ideas

A new product can consist of technological innovation or simple repackaging. It can come from an improvement in quality or a decrease in cost. It can be tangible, like a microwave oven, or intangible, like a new system of meditation. It can be a manufacturing process, like the assembly line, or a biochemical process, like gene splicing. It can be revolutionary or evolutionary.

New products can result from renaming, restyling, recombining, or giving old products new advertising slants. They can be modernized ways of supplying existing services,

23

such as overnight parcel delivery, credit cards, and automated tellers. They can be useful, pleasurable, profitable, fun, healthful, convenient, gimmicky, labor-saving, or any combination of these.

A new product can be an actual thing or service, or it can be a different promotional strategy for an existing item. Its "newness" can come from manufacturing or marketing. Although there is usually an overlap, this dichotomy provides a helpful way of thinking about specific concepts.

The checklist in this chapter yields ideas for tangible new products. The list in Chapter 3 produces concepts based primarily on merchandising or promotional elements. Both checklists lay down dozens of runways for your creativity to take off. Once your imagination starts to soar, these lists will keep you in new product ideas indefinitely. Although many of them will sound silly, this is only the take-off. Landing back on earth comes later.

It is good to mix thinking and doing. Don't feel you have to read these checklists straight through. If you feel exhausted or overloaded, stop and do one of the exercises in Chapter 4 or doodle in your notebook.

√ **Solve a problem.** It may be complex, but it could also be as simple as catching a fish or frying an egg. The world is full of both major difficulties and minor inconveniences. What would eliminate one of them? The solution could be deceptively easy, or it could require extensive research.

Consider first aid. How many times have you wished for a bandage that was easily applied with one hand, without any fussy little wrappers to undo? There is a "hole" in the market for just such a product. Could you invent and design a cartridge-loaded bandage dispenser that is operated with only one hand? Would you call it "One-Arm Band-Its"? Will it look like a miniature slot machine? Pull the crank and out the bottom comes your jackpot in the form of a sterile ready-to-apply bandage.

You could have several versions: practical models for home and school; streamlined designer dispensers for the office; vending machines for stores, shops, and public places; and portable models. There could even be select-a-size features. All will come with a supply of sterile refill cartridges, which will be sold separately. The cartridges will be the real money-makers, year after year, once every home and office has a one-arm bandage dispenser.

√ **Apply a new technology in an unrelated field.** Digital readouts, first used in calculators and watches, now show up in any product that utilizes numbers—thermometers, scales, billboards, and bus destination signs. Small solar energy panels now power calculators and watches. Computers are found in copiers, cars, stereos, and ovens, and they may soon be in clothing to remind you to zip your fly.

How about inventing a new method for compatible individuals to meet? Our high-tech world creates so much alienation and impersonality that it is difficult to find really special friends and lovers. Why not use technology to *assist* people in this? The first computer dating service, Operation Match, was launched in 1965 by three Harvard College students, including one of the authors of this book. Today the concept is still going strong as hundreds of computer dating companies help people find their ideal mates. The idea has been elaborated into video dating services, television and radio dating game shows, and national computer dating databases.

Still, there is much room for further refinement. How about individually-programmed computer chips linked to tiny radio transceivers that send and receive personal information? These electronic auras could be called "Friend Chips." When two mutually compatible people came within a certain distance, their "Friend Chips" would begin to buzz or vibrate, and this would increase in intensity the closer they got. These high-tech, people-matching machines would enable potential friends and lovers to home in on each other. "Friend Chips" would be worn like beepers, or, ideally, in more miniaturized form, as jewelry. If either party decided not to go through with the introduction, he or she could push a decoy button to shut off the system.

Could this new product idea be a breakthrough for enhancing relationships? Maybe it should be called "Relation Chips." Will people object that it is too inhuman and alienating to produce meaningful interaction? Do these same people object to using the telephone?

The concept is also appropriate for locating lost children or pets.

√ **Think of an accessory for the latest in technology.** Technical expertise is not mandatory. Computers are a classic case in point. They have spawned disk files, paper holders, carrying cases, and all types of special furniture and esoteric accoutrements. It did not take a computer genius to invent these products. All it required was observing how these magical machines are used and thinking of ways to make them more comfortable or efficient.

Can you dream up a new piece of computer hardware? Many machines and appliances have foot pedals, so why not invent one for computers? You could call it "Ground Control" and design it as a cursor mover and scrolling device. Or you may go crazy with the concept and invent an elaborate platform and instrument panel for foot- and leg-operated functions. It could be raised and slanted at just the right angle to serve as a comfortable foot rest. Why not make it totally adjustable? Promote it as the new-age accessory for making computer operations wholistic as well as downright comfortable.

Similarly, what accessories could ride the popularity of video cassette recorders, credit cards, and automated teller machines? Think for a moment what a vast influence the credit card has had. It was merely a new product idea twenty years ago.

How about miniature rear-view mirrors for ATM users to keep others from peeking at their secret codes and private transactions? Or perhaps the mirrors would provide a sense of security to nighttime pedestrians in strange neighborhoods. The name could play on the well-known phrase, "eyes in the back of your head."

√ **Find a simpler solution.** Even if a problem has been solved, there may be an easier way. Getting champagne to ferment in the bottle is complex and costly. The simpler bulk process was invented to put the bubbly into bottles *after* fermentation has begun in vats. The product is just as good, and the price is much lower.

√ **Put an existing product to another use.** The Chemex coffee maker was created by chemists who brought a basic filtration system out of the lab and into the kitchen. Other products might require more extensive modifications and restyling in order to fit their new uses. For example, there is now an electronic fertility monitor for women. It was adapted from a device used for predicting ovulation in horses and cows.

√ **Change the purpose or function of a product.** Beepers are used to contact people and alert them to get messages. You can now purchase a phony beeper, which will go off whenever you choose. It can be used to impress others or to escape boring meetings without providing excuses. Will general awareness of these False Alarms render them useless or, perhaps, bring about an overhaul of the code of beeper ethics? "Beep unto others as you would have others beep unto you."

√ **Alter the scale of something.** Small windmills have been used for centuries, primarily to pump water. Today, giant wind turbines are installed in windy areas to generate sizable amounts of electricity. What other things could lend themselves to a change in scale?

√ **Think of things to save time.** The market for convenience items is unlimited—at work, at home, in childcare, in handling personal finances, in gardening, in automobile repair, and practically everywhere else. A staple of modern family life, prepared baby food, was invented in the 1920s by Dan Gerber when he learned how much his wife hated the task of straining adult foods for their baby. There are hundreds of other examples. TV dinners are perhaps the supreme convenience items.

What other goods or services would appeal to workaholics and others who feel a time crunch? How about something for working mothers? Someone recently invented a clothes-shopping service for professional women. Can you come up with a convenient way for citizens to communicate with their political leaders? An instant "Letter to the President"?

√ **Devise something disposable.** Can you think of a new product to eliminate cleaning or simplify maintenance? It doesn't have to be as fancy as the frostless refrigerator or the self-cleaning oven. Disposable diapers are the end-all example.

√ **Adapt an existing product for use in a new setting.** TVs, bars, and telephones have moved into autos. Perhaps garbage disposals and paper shredders will follow. Video games and biofeedback devices have traveled to wrist watches. Clocks are now found in computers and VCRs. All sorts of things have moved to the person and become individualized or mobile—the stereo, the personal computer, the portable copier, and the mobile telephone. What will be next?

√ **Invent an item for a specific manufacturer.** Take any existing product and think of a similar item or something that could be used with it. Perhaps you will come up with an idea you can sell to the manufacturer as a line extension or accessory.

A recent new product success is the self-adhesive cushion which provides a soft telephone rest for the shoulder. Would the manufacturer be interested in a line of soft stick-on corners for furniture in homes with toddlers? They could come in various shapes, sizes, and colors.

√ **Delete a feature that is thought to be essential.** Several companies sell books with blank pages for use as diaries, private editions of poetry, and so on. Another example is cassette tapes that play "silence," or "white noise."

√ **Invent a food.** Make something else out of chocolate. Change a flavor. Make an existing brand lighter. Or heavier. Take something traditional and give it a contemporary taste or appearance. Change the way a food is packaged or sold. Make a diet version of something otherwise forbidden, like cheesecake or chocolate soda. Make something healthier—delete or reduce the salt, the caffeine, the sugar, or the calories.

Put a popular flavor into a popular food. Salad dressing is a multi-billion-dollar-a-year product category. Many people like mushrooms in salads. Although the concept was introduced a few years ago, there is currently no mushroom-flavor salad dressing on the market.

Take a popular street food, like soft pretzels or falafel, and package it for sale on a larger scale. Invent a new line of ethnic fast foods. It's been done with tacos. Why not Indian curries?

√ **Model a health food after a mainstream favorite, or vice versa.** Several years ago it was difficult to find any good-tasting treats in the natural food stores. There was a hole in the market. One of the first delicious, yet healthful, candy bars was

"Good Karmal," developed by one of the authors. It was consciously designed to be like the best-selling Snickers, but to have more flavor and no sugar, preservatives, or artificial ingredients. Good Karmal was a pioneer health-and-naturals product in the use of designer packaging and merchandising techniques.

Ironically, many mainstream products are now designed with down-home looks and marketed as "natural" or "organic" to exploit the health and fitness craze. It is almost to the point where you can no longer tell the products by their uniforms.

√ **Make something instant.** Take a difficult food to prepare, such as fudge, and make it simple. Ready-to-use pressed garlic is a good example. You can now buy special salt for making Margueritas. About three cents worth is packaged in containers made for easily coating the rims of glasses. The cost to consumers is about a dollar.

√ **Cook up something for new eating styles.** The home yogurt maker was developed after health foods became popular. How about a device for making veggie burgers out of tofu?

√ **Revive an old-fashioned food.** Do so either by selling the food itself or the equipment to make it. A recent example is a set for making rosette pastries.

√ **Invent a kitchen gadget.** Create a utensil for a newly popularized food. How about a kiwi-fruit peeler? A tofu storage container? Visit a trade show for gourmet foods and kitchen products. Walk the aisles. Select something and start brainstorming items to use with it. Choose a gadget and see if it could be applied to other foods. Can you design an automatic sauce stirrer?

√ **Improve an existing product.** Find something that does not work well, analyze what is wrong with it, and change it. IBM created the type ball to improve the effectiveness of typewriters and allow interchangeable typefaces. The automatic correction ribbon and memory typewriters soon followed.

√ **Change the form of an existing product.** If it is lotion, make it spray-on. If it is powder, create a cream. Change bars to chunks, granules to flakes, solids to liquids.

√ **Invent a toy or game.** Can you think of a new design or angle for a toy, a doll, a puzzle? It should be emphasized that these are, along with clothes, some of the most difficult categories to break into with new products. Still, there are good prospects. "Action toys" are often created with boys in mind, but girls may be just as receptive, particularly if the toys represent appealing role models. Likewise, boys enjoy dolls or cooking-related toys if presented in a nonstereotypical manner. Sex roles are becoming less rigidly defined and the loosening can be a source of opportunity for creating new products.

√ **Change an existing toy.** Add a light, change the material, make it glow in the dark, give it moveable parts or an accessory, change the size, make it educational, or add or delete sound effects. Of course, you cannot copy any protected products, but you may be able to use their underlying premises as a springboard for your own playtime concepts.

√ **Think of a new automobile gadget.** There are millions of cars. Someone invented a spray to make any automobile smell new inside. Someone else invented spill-proof commuter coffee cups. They were originally designed for use on sailboats, but are now selling like hotcakes for autos.

Can you think of some way to keep maps organized? An emergency road kit? A safe, practical directory for drivers with car phones? A hiding place for valuables? An easy-to-use maintenance reminder? Almost everyone likes house plants, so how about Car Plants? Would they have to be cacti, to withstand the heat? The advertising slogan could be, "Support an American Car Plant." Will the Japanese retaliate with "Automobanzai"?

√ **Invent something specifically for commuters.** How could the time be more enjoyably spent in autos or public transport? How could people be warned of delays or informed of alternate routes when accidents occur? How can they find convenient carpools?

√ **Create a safety device.** There is a huge potential market for such products for children, homes, cars, hotel rooms, women on the street, and so on. The devices can relate to fire, theft, personal safety, or retrieval of stolen property. For example, a Massachusetts man recently invented a radio transmitter for installation in automobiles. It emits a signal which can be activated and tracked by the police when a car is reported stolen.

How about instant oxygen for high-rise buildings? When these towers catch fire, most of the injuries and deaths are from smoke inhalation. Portable tanks containing thirty-minute oxygen supplies could be made available throughout tall buildings. Could they save countless lives? Or would the flammable oxygen be more dangerous than the smoke? Don't stop your brainstorming to worry about that now.

√ **Adapt an existing service.** Make it available on a temporary or fill-in basis. Part-time clerical workers have existed for years. Now there are temporary accountants and lawyers who work during others' vacations and periods of increased business. Such services appeal both to the employers, who do not have to pay full-time salaries, and to employees, who can maintain flexible schedules.

Gift registries, traditionally used by brides, are being tried for singles setting up their households. Another new service assists companies recruiting new employees by introducing prospects' spouses to possible employers, civic groups, and other local facilities in order to encourage the entire family's support for the move.

√ **Introduce something purely informational.** What are you an expert in? Can you cook up a new theory of pop psychology, relaxation, or stress reduction? Do you have a diet plan that is as good or better than the hundreds of other existing systems? Turn your special knowledge into a book, a cassette, a video tape, or a seminar.

Maybe you have a collection of wise and witty quotations. You could write a short book of wisdom entitled *The Golden and Other Rules*. Everyone knows the Golden Rule. But how many people know the Aluminum Rule? "When the rising curve of confidence meets the declining curve of skill, the stage is set for a truly monumental learning experience." Maybe it is not a book, but a line of greeting cards. There are many ways to develop an idea. How about the Gasoline Rule? "When in doubt, floor it."

√ **Unleash an idea for pet owners.** People spend large amounts of money on their pets. The average dog costs its owner about $800 per year, and the average cat costs just under $400. What about something for owners and pets to play with, or a gadget to facilitate feeding and watering?

You could make a machine that talks to lonesome animals while their owners are out. It could play a bark-, meow-, or chirp-activated cassette of master talking or singing, including all the silly things he or she always says to Fido, Cleo, or Polly. It could be called "My Master's Voice," or better, "The Great Pet Tender." It would come with a cassette of the Platters' hit song from the fifties, "The Great

Pretender." The fifties are "in" now, especially the use of fifties tunes to market products to Baby Boomers. Also, the words of "The Great Pretender" fit the function of "The Great Pet Tender" perfectly. Purchasers could record their own messages or music over the Platters or on the other side of the tape.

√ **Come up with a product for neighbors of pet owners.** What about the problem of loud dogs? Could you create a device that sends painful high-pitched sounds directly at an offending canine? Or could you devise something simpler, based on pleasure rather than pain, such as popped corn cereal repackaged in a box labeled "Dog Silencers"? A handful of these super-sweet breakfast balls has been known to silence several backyard bowsers. Perhaps it would work on others.

√ **Create an item for some specific consumer behavior.** People love to read the backs of cereal boxes. Why not take advantage of this? Create illustrated adventure and romance stories and serialize them for publication on boxes of breakfast foods. Call them "Cereal Serials." Make them so exciting that people consume cereal more rapidly in order to get each new installment. They could be based on educational, sports, health, and various other topics. Perhaps the whole concept will be called "Corn Flake College" and include coupons and box tops to redeem for diplomas, school-type fashions, and other appropriate accoutrements.

As Corn Flake College succeeds, perhaps you will expand to "Soap Operas" on the backs of detergent boxes. What next? "Pet Rock Concerts" in the form of free cassettes packed inside the larger sizes of pet food containers? These could be used on any tape player, but would be designed especially for The Great Pet Tender.

√ **Invent a new type of package.** The "aseptically packaged" juices in boxes, which were developed in Europe, are cheaper to package, ship, and store, and they are convenient for on-the-go consumers. Remember the revolution created by the pop top? The originators of such systems can reap significant financial reward.

Think of a new way to automate existing packaging. Shrink-wrap and the machine that automatically ties strings around boxes in bakeries replaced manual wrapping. Is there any way to bag groceries automatically?

√ **Study the trends.** This is a good way to identify and select likely product categories for your brainstorming. Make a list of major social changes on both the national and personal levels.

The list might include: the health-and-naturals movement; the tendency of people to delay marriage and childbirth; the changing housekeeping standards as more women work outside the home; the increases in single-parent households; the growing number of people making career changes; the rise in working women in both traditional and nontraditional categories; the concern with pollution and waste management; the desire to balance career and personal life; the need for personal fulfillment and stress reduction; the shift from the industrial revolution to the communication revolution; and many others. Let your imagination loose among these trends.

√ **Have a brainchild for the current baby boom.** Annual births are up from a low of just over three million per year in the early seventies to approximately four million per year in the mid-eighties. Invent a product to make travel with children easier, facilitate child care, or enhance early education. What about new-age solutions to traditional problems, such as nutrition and diaper rash? Natural baby food and natural-fiber diaper covers are now available.

Annual sales of baby products are about $12 billion and growing. Two-career parents are reportedly spending an average of about twenty thousand dollars on each child before he or she enters kindergarten!

√ **Uncork an idea for the wine craze.** What products would appeal to people just learning about wine? To connoisseurs? Several successful new wine-related products are wine coolers, light wine, nonalcoholic wine, wine racks, wine chillers, wine carrying cases, and so on. How about associating nonwine products with wine? There are now Chardonnay bouquet soaps, Zinfandel bubble baths, and gimmick wine bottles full of everything from soup to nuts.

√ **Come up with items for popular leisure activities.** Can you add an accessory to some sporting gear? Design a carrier for a particular piece of equipment? Create a device for the fitness craze? The inventors of the Soloflex and Nautilus machines have made millions.

The most popular means of exercise in the United States is walking. Has this relatively unexciting activity been overlooked? How about a product especially for walkers? The potential market is astronomical. Is this how Sony's Walkman was originally envisioned?

Can you create a new sports activity, with a product to go along? An enterprising racquetball club manager came up with "wallyball" to increase the use of the indoor courts. By stringing a volleyball net across a walled racquetball court and finding a ball suitable to bounce off the walls, a new sport was born, complete with a national tournament.

What will replace the Frisbee? What will come after the skateboard? What will you get if you combine them?

√ **What is the perfect product for the spiritual and religious market?** Can you find it? Get inspired. What about the revival of fundamentalist religion? What products would further the values and goals of believers? How about computer-designed icons or worship services on video cassettes?

√ **Examine your own life.** What recent changes have occurred? Look at your family life, your social life, and the lives of your friends, children, and associates. What new products or services do those changes suggest?

√ **Look around your home.** Is there some problem you want to solve? How could energy be saved? What would remind family members to turn off lights and appliances?

Pretend you are a visitor from a different culture and observe all of your familiar possessions from a changed perspective. What do you see? What is all this stuff? Do you own too much? Is the clutter in your way or tying you down? Are others similarly afflicted? How about a special cleaning company to help people organize their lives? You could call your customized uncluttering service "Clean For a Day." The slogan could be, "Cling forever or clean for a day."

√ **How have decorating trends changed?** The popularity of mini-blinds has prompted special gadgets for cleaning them. What products might be useful to owners of hardwood floors or redwood decks? Can you think of new approaches to lighting?

√ **What can you mix up to preserve and maintain popular materials?** There has been increased use of wood and leather at home, work, and play. How about one product for treating and preserving both? Mineral oil is such a product. It can be used to beautify, protect, and preserve all wood surfaces that are not already waxed. It is also excellent for conditioning all leathers except suede. Mineral oil is the primary ingredient in many moisturizers and the only ingredient in most baby oils. It is one of the best body oils you can buy. Design an attractive package for this all-purpose product and call it "Rubitín." The accent mark gives it a European designer flair. The name is descriptive. It invites people to "rub it in" to their wood and leather treasures, treating and conditioning their hands in the process.

√ **Look some more.** What things do you see that are found not only in your home, but also in virtually every other house in the country? How about the paper towel dispenser? Can you think of some way to adapt this universal unit to make it do more? Could it become a holder for the one-arm bandages? Is this an opportunity for an extension of "Corn Flake College" into printed paper towels? If it's a success, they'll really be on a roll.

√ **What are the trends in beauty supplies and toiletries?** Are women looking for more cosmetics or different hair care products, such as gels and mousses? Could they come in more convenient containers or be dispensed differently? What about another "fun" cosmetic like glitter for the hair or green nail polish?

Don't forget men. Males are using more and more cosmetics and toiletries of all kinds. Gillette recently introduced a "shaving system" that combines a brush with its own internal supply of lather. What other toiletry gadgets might appeal to males?

√ **Aim just ahead of the present.** What forces brought about the current trends? What else might result from such forces? You want to be the first to hit on the ideal product for the next trend. You want to greet it with *the* luxury or necessity, or both. What is just on the horizon? If you aim too close to the present, the next trend will go by without you. And if you are too far-seeing, you will miss it, a penniless prophet.

√ **What people have been ignored in the marketplace?** Has anyone really explored the needs of the handicapped, singles, teenagers, allergic people, the elderly, commuters, homeowners, grandparents, and parents with children in college? For example, think through the needs of men as single fathers or housekeepers. What about "male" cleaning products, cooking utensils, baby care lines, and so on?

Don't forget people in temporary roles or situations. Could you design a convenient change-of-address kit for people who are moving? Remember how frustrating it is to have to write out your old and new addresses for all your subscriptions, charge accounts, friends, and memberships? Maybe you could develop a set of cards and a rubber stamp to print both addresses at once. You could try to sell the idea to a moving company or a national franchise of printing shops.

√ **Investigate the implications of two-income families.** Not only is there more disposable income in such families, but the pattern of *who* does the buying may have changed. Do working women send their teenagers to do the shopping? Can you think of a product to sell to these teens in grocery stores?

Each year, Americans spend approximately $150 million on acne medications. Why not design a new one with a catchy name that sounds less medicinal than the pimple products presently on the market? You could package it in a can under the name "Spot Remover." Perhaps humor is inappropriate for such a sensitive problem. Better try a package with a pretty face instead, calling the product "Save Face." How about one "specially formulated" for girls and another for boys?

√ **What are the ramifications of more households with senior citizens?** What could help solve their special problems, such as manipulating fasteners for shoes and clothes, reaching things on shelves, cleaning the house, opening medicine bottles and other containers, reading small print, and getting purchases from store to home? There are now employment agencies exclusively for the elderly. What other new goods or services would cater not only to the needs of these older persons, but also to the needs of their housemates?

√ **Are families getting larger or smaller?** People are having fewer children per family, but many children are living at home longer. They are even bringing their own families back to live with their parents. What could be used by these new extended families? How about things to help feed more people, increase privacy, or make it easier to share the bathroom? Could you invent an instant second sink for the family bathroom? It could be designed to connect quickly to an existing sink and hang easily on almost any wall. A bowl, some plastic tubing, a few clamps, inventive packaging—Voila! You have a runaway best-selling new product. The slogan is, "Insta-Sinks Install Instantly."

√ **"Segment" a product.** Take an item that is consumed by a large part of the population. Can that market be segmented by changing the product in some way to make it more appealing to a subgroup? Many foods have been segmented into salt-free, sugar-free, light, organic, and natural versions, plus various combinations of these, each with its own adherents.

Also consider shoes. From the sneakers of the fifties, we now have running shoes, aerobics shoes, basketball shoes, racquetball shoes, tennis shoes, shoes ad infinitum. What is next?

√ **Dream up something that may be used by everyone.** Everybody sleeps. Can you create a product to enhance sleep? A dream-generating machine or pillow? Kava Kava tea has a reputation for inducing epic nighttime reveries. Could you fill a pillow with some and call it "Dream On"? How about a new method of waking up? A new type of alarm clock, possibly? A catapult system? A last-resort cold-water sprinkler to get you up after you have pushed the snooze button once too often? It could be called "Dunk Beds." Are these throw-away gags or valuable ideas for keeping? Maybe they are both. Don't worry about it now. Just write them down. You can decide later.

√ **Capitalize on a craze.** Trivia has proven to be a long-lasting fad. How about turning this entire concept inside-out and producing a game called "Meaningful Pursuits"? You could spin off a whole line of related products built around themes such as ecology, religion, peace, health, and so on.

√ **Come up with a gimmick.** Gadgets and novelties can be phenomenal successes or dismal failures. All but the most spectacular gimmick successes will be short-lived. You might try something like "American Incense." Put three charcoal briquets in a baggie and staple a label across the top. On one side of the label print, "*AMERICAN INCENSE,*" and on the other, "*Instructions:* 1) Soak in kerosene, 2) Light."

√ **Look for similarities and relationships between seemingly unlike things.** Baseball players chew gum and tobacco. Someone packaged shredded bubble gum in pouches similar to those used for chewing tobacco. They are selling very well under the name "Big League Chew."

A smoker looked at a blowtorch and got the idea for the pocket butane lighter. These have been selling for years by the millions.

√ **Think about some common chore.** What could make it easier, cleaner, more fun, or more healthy? How about a new way to light charcoal that would eliminate the unsavory instant chemicals and smelly fluids? You could design a blowtorch in the shape of a six-shooter. It could have a built-in igniter and butane refill cartridges in the shape of bullets. When you want to light a fire, simply point the gun at the charcoal, pull the trigger, and, presto, instant flame.

√ **Look around your neighborhood.** Does this stimulate any thoughts? Almost every home has a barbeque. How about an accessory for these omnipresent pits of uncontrollable smoke and flame? Can you invent a way of getting the smoke to blow any direction you wish, say, away from you and your friends, and towards unwanted guests? What about the flames, which are so hard to start and then so difficult to control? How about adapting a plastic plant mister for cooling the fire when it threatens the meat? Will you call it "Mist For The Grill"? How will you keep it from melting?

Perhaps that name is not right. Perhaps the mister is not right either. Maybe a good old squirt gun specially designed for the purpose would be better. It could be a super-long-range model so you could blast a runaway barbeque fire from your easy chair, from the volleyball court, or even from second base. You could design a special holster and four-gun set for the professional: One gun for fluid, the second to start the flame, the third one for water, and the fourth for your favorite sauce.

√ **Create something for heavy users of another product.** What accessories might be bought by heavy smokers or drinkers? If the heavy use itself causes problems, what might alleviate them? For smokers, there is special toothpaste. For drinkers, there are individually-packaged breath analysis tests for the purse or pocket.

How about a "Pack of Lies" for "the smoker in your life"? It would be designed in the size and shape of a pack of cigarettes. Inside are twenty little pieces of paper rolled up in the shape of cigarettes. Each of these little scrolls has a different "lie" printed on it. When you take them out and unroll them, you find sayings such as: "Barring a national disaster, or some other act of God, this is the last one I'll ever smoke;" "Smoking is good for me;" "A cigarette early in the morning opens my lungs and helps me breathe;" "Real life consists of those boring moments between cigarettes;" "Smoking improves my sexual potency;" and so on.

√ **Learn from mistakes.** Whether they are yours or someone else's, mistakes often provide valuable information. Learn to take advantage of serendipity and coincidence. When you goof or don't get what you are expecting, examine what you *did* get. This pragmatic approach has led to a number of successful new products.

For example, Ivory Soap was "invented" when a mixing machine was left on accidentally and the resulting batch of soap floated. It was an instant hit. Scotchguard was another accident turned into high profitability. Someone unwittingly spilled the chemical on a tennis shoe. Testing revealed that it resisted dirt, and it is now a best-selling soil and stain repellent for carpets and fabrics. Maybe you could clean up on a mistake, too.

The point is, if something does not work the way you planned, don't throw it out, but examine what it *will* do. It may be far better than what you were hoping for.

√ **Talk with people.** Have you contracted the germ of a new product idea, but don't know how it will develop, how you might spread it, or whether it could become contagious? Confide in a few people you know. Ask if they can see any use for your idea in their own lives or lines of work. For example, if you have thought of a way to hold things together without zippers, buttons, snaps, rivets, bolts, glue, or other traditional fasteners, find out how it could be useful in different areas. Ask a cross section of friends and associates how your idea could make life easier for them. Holding things together is important. What will you call your miracle product? "Instant Gravity"?

√ **Revive an old product.** Many things come and go in cycles. Think how certain products and services change over time. What former favorites have fallen into disuse? Can they be upscaled or improved and reintroduced? Such "new" products can be quite successful. For example, after many years of nonproduction, convertibles are making a smash comeback in the American automobile industry.

Perhaps the best example of product recycling is the fat-tired bicycle. Comfy big-tired bikes were almost totally replaced by the sexy ten-speeds, which were not as comfortable or as safe. Now the old clunkers are back, spiffed up as "mountain bikes" and promoted with trendy ads.

√ **Make something out of waste.** Could you cook up a joint venture between a cookie company and a chocolate manufacturer? They would use broken cookies as "chips" in chocolate bars—big, delicious chocolate-chip cookies turned inside out. Such "Cookie Chip Chocolates" could be sold in gourmet cookie stores and chocolate boutiques. They could even be mass-marketed nationally.

√ **Can waste be prevented or materials used more efficiently?** There is waste produced in any manufacturing situation. Can it be prevented? Can it be utilized in some way to make another product?

√ **Think of a sensational name.** Sometimes you will come up with great names and then devise products to fit. Consider the name "Paydirt." Can you dig up some things which might profitably utilize this great name, such as mulch or kitty litter made out of shredded greenbacks?

√ **Use popular phrases.** Turn an everyday word or popular phrase into a brand name. Your new product will be well recognized the instant it is released. You may realize free benefits of years of familiarity equivalent to millions of dollars of free advertising.

The fabric softener Bounce is an example of successfully turning a common word or well-known phrase into a product name. The strategy works best when you have a great product idea, such as fabric softener for the *dryer*, to market under a great name.

Take the phrase "French kiss." Could you connect two chocolate kisses and call the merger a "French Kiss"? How would you package such a suggestive product? How would you market it? "To be consumed by lovers, one at each end," of course.

Perhaps you could develop a line of baking mixes under the name "Scratch." With this product, when asked where the pastry came from, the host or hostess could smile and say, in all honesty, "I made it from Scratch!"

√ **Synthesize two or more services.** Many large companies are now trying to combine every conceivable financial service under one roof. What great combos can you think up? Maybe a shop selling pastries and classical records called "The Bachery"?

√ **Brainstorm for a time-specific product.** Think of something that could be related to a specific time—day, night, morning, weekend, lunchtime, whenever. Cold remedies have been around for years, but Nyquill was the first to be promoted as the nighttime remedy. Then there's "Miller Time." Devise other products that have their own times. The strategy works.

√ **Alter a material.** Sometimes a mere change in material can completely alter the nature of something. What new materials are in vogue? Gore-tex, Titanium, Mylar, parachute fabric? These can make old fashioned products appear high-tech. Canvas sports shoes became altogether new when made of nylon and special foam. They developed further with air soles and miracle fabrics.

√ **Present information in a new way.** Many museums offer radios or cassette players with earphones for people to hear guided tours while seeing exhibits at their own pace. This idea is now being used for audio and video cassettes of all kinds, including commuter colleges and tourist attractions. A California company adapted this concept for automobile cassette guides to various wine-growing areas of Northern California. They feature narrations of an area's history and attractions and are of interest both to local residents and motoring tourists. Turning the concept around, you can have the tour come to hospital patients, prisoners, or other immobile consumers. For instance, you can now buy videotapes of bike routes to watch while riding an exercycle.

√ **Make something safer.** There are many products on the market that are somewhat hazardous to use. How could they be made less so? By changing the product? The dispenser? The method of use? Does something need to be child-proofed? How could this be accomplished?

√ **Study successful new products.** What made them winners? Examine especially the current hits. What lessons do they reveal about present trends and consumer preferences? How can these insights be applied in other areas? Think back to before they hit the market. What cultural clues can you find that could have led to the ideas behind their creation? Can you spot any similar hints now? What clues to tomorrow are contained in today's culture?

√ **Study a business.** Select a store, a service, an industry, or a business. It can be one with which you are familiar or one that is entirely new to you. Research it by talking with people, reading relevant trade magazines and books, and visiting facilities. How does it operate? Are there any ways in which it could be made more efficient, more pleasurable, more convenient? What factors contribute to its smooth operation? What shortcuts are used? What are the tricks of the trade? Can any of those elements be applied to another business or industry?

√ **Visit a factory.** See how something is made. Observe and admire the incredible machinery. What does it resemble? What else could it make? What other materials could it handle?

Find out what manufacturers are in your area. There are many companies which only make "private label" products for others to merchandise and sell. Sears does not make any products directly. It has them made by others or by companies in which it has an ownership interest. You can do the same. Or perhaps you can produce something *for* a company like Sears. The point is, learn what is going on out there.

Over 2500 plants, mines, agencies, banks, and other business, cultural, and educational organizations that offer tours are listed in Gale Research's *Tours and Visits Directory*. Tours of other facilities can often be arranged simply by asking.

√ **Consider industrial products.** Do not limit your thinking to consumer products. Industries are constantly looking for new products and ideas for improvements, as well as ways to make production cleaner and cheaper. Likewise, agriculture can always utilize new concepts that provide higher returns.

People already in an industry are the most knowledgeable about it, and they are often willing to share their thoughts on how things might be improved. They may even wish to work with you if your concept catches their fancy. This could give you access to vital technical assistance and contacts within the company or industry.

√ **Look for holes in the market.** Search for things which do not exist but for which there would be buyers. Try to identify, or target, unique classes of consumers. You might even discover an emerging buying group and develop an entire line of products for it. Going beyond existing areas, and actually creating *new* categories, is a major achievement. It can be very rewarding, both intellectually and monetarily.

The above checklist is by no means complete. But it is certain to get some ideas flowing. And once you let them get started, they will continue to come and multiply on their own.

CHAPTER 3: GETTING IDEAS THAT ARE PRIMARILY PROMOTIONAL

The **Goochy Goo** *Chronicles*

It's a sure thing! A new petroleum jelly to compete with Vaseline. Just being next to it on the shelves will give my new product more credibility than I could buy for millions of dollars of advertising. I'll have a much handsomer package and a far superior name, something less medicinal and more descriptive. I think I will get these expensive little tubes after all. Study 'em. Stroll the old supermarket aisles and ponder this . . . . . Vasel—, I mean, petrolatum. What a marvelously versatile product: first aid, make-up remover, lubricant, pipe goop—oh brother, I have to go finish that sink—diaper rash treatment. The list is endless. Just goop it on. Wait a second. Goop." What a name! But it's been done—hand cleaner. Hmmm, "Goo." That's a better one. No—it's for baby—"Goochy Goo." That's better yet. In fact, it's a great name. It's descriptive, plus it's already a well-known household expression, which means the advertising won't be as expensive. It will come in a designer package, but cost less than Vaseline. This is gonna be a sure thing . . . . . ♩♫♪ Thank heaven for broken sinks . . . . . ♩♩♫

49

Remember the old adage, "Necessity is the mother of invention"? A traditional method of new product development is to "find a need and fill it." But modern marketing has demonstrated that there are different types of needs. Some are not true necessities at all, but we often come to perceive them as such.

These are things we want or believe we must have for a variety of reasons: They are familiar; they are convenient; they confer status; or they simply make life enjoyable. Marketing can create consumers' perception of these as needs. In such cases one could say that "invention is the mother of necessity." The merchandising of a product comes first, and the "need" for it follows.

Most new products require promotion. But sometimes marketing tactics can, in themselves, constitute new products. Existing items can be "new" or "improved" with repackaging or a shift in advertising slant, while the actual products remain virtually the same. Of course, such newness alone is no guarantee of success. The most successful, longest-lived goods and services—the "great ideas" of the world—are often those that combine honest and ingenious *marketing* concepts with beneficial and genuine *products*.

The following checklist presents some ways of getting ideas that are new primarily in marketing or promotional content. The dividing line between the items in this chapter and those in the preceding one is not always clearcut. Many ideas can fit into either list, and sometimes both. Do not worry about classifying your concepts. Just use the lists to help your imagination take flight.

Checklist for Getting New Product Ideas That Have a Strong Marketing or Promotional Element

√ **Put an old product in a new package.** Remember cherry colas, fountain style? There is an entire generation that has never had one. Coca Cola's introduction of Cherry Coke is a good example of this marketing strategy. Perhaps Chocolate Coke, Vanilla

Coke, and all the other former favorite fountain flavors will follow.

Maybe you could just market the syrups. Design a little six-pack of best-selling soft drink syrups, call it "The Old Fashioned Soda Shoppe" and sell it for use with club soda and ice cream. People could concoct their own creations at home.

√ **Design a unique dispenser.** A new product is often nothing more than a new container. A popular new product dispenses nail polish in a stick. It is clean and easy and allows users to draw and write on their nails almost anywhere.

A new lip moisturizer recently hit the market with a rolling applicator. Will people associate it with underarm deodorants and balk at using it on their lips? Or will it become a best seller?

How about combining *two* applicators? Bissell did so with its Upholstery Shampoo that combines a spray can and a brush.

√ **Jazz up a boring or staid product.** Tie it in with something trendy, like fitness. Take athlete's foot preparations out of their medicinal packages and put them in smart, colorful containers.

"Stinky Pinkys" are attractively packaged odor-absorbers for athletic shoes. Previously, such products were hidden in plain wrappers in the medical products sections of pharmacies. Now they are prominently displayed in sporting goods and various other type stores.

√ **Create with colors.** Colors and patterns go in and out of style. Pink and black emerged as a trendy combination in the fifties, became passé, and resurfaced in the eighties. Remember the paisley ties of the sixties? You can create a new product simply by changing the color, pattern, or texture of something.

√ **Make a luxury item generic, or vice versa.** Research why cosmetics and perfumes are so expensive. Most are manufactured from inexpensive ingredients, including dirt, dyes, basic chemicals, little brushes, sponges, pencils, and so on.

Much is spent on marketing to create the right image for these luxury items, while their actual ingredients are quite simple and inexpensive. The fancy designer packaging and promotional materials are part of what makes them cost so much. But still, the mark-ups are often enormous.

Could you create a line of generic cosmetics? Many designer products are identical to generics except for the packaging and promotion. They are sometimes produced by the same manufacturers, who simply change the labels, sometimes in the middle of a production run.

Maybe you could combine the designer and generic concepts into a new brand. How about calling it "Designer Generics"? All the graphics and labels would be half designer and half generic, so that each package is part fancy and part plain. You would give consumers the choice of paying a designer or generic amount. Your slogan could be "Pay Either Price," and you could print both prices right on the package. This would give consumers the ultimate in freedom of choice. They would thus be able to select image or value and know exactly what they were getting for their money.

√ **Extend a brand.** Companies often create new products with "brand extensions" by simply putting an established brand name on other items. A good example is Hershey's Chocolate Milk. Consumers associate the "new" product with the familiar name and may be more inclined to purchase it.

You may be able to utilize brand extension in a small way if you have a well-accepted product of your own and want to add another. You also may be able to suggest a brand extension to an existing manufacturer.

A well-known brand name does not guarantee success. It can, in fact, create an undesirable association. For example, Campbell's Soups came out with a spaghetti sauce billed as "Campbell's Very Own Special Sauce." It was a failure because the name "Campbell's" conjured up an image of thin, soupy tomato sauce that was not at all appealing to pasta connoisseurs. Today millions of people buy the same special sauce under the name "Prego."

√ **Combine a well-known name and a unique container.** How about a new snack called "The Leaning Tower of Pizza"? Design a container in the shape of the famous Tower of Pisa. The bottom will be on an angle so that the package leans on the shelf. Inside are pizza-flavored cheese puffs.

√ **Take something from one product category and put it into another.** Large cereal makers have taken granola out of backpackers' breakfast bowls and profitably put it into their fast-selling, super-sweet, candy bars.

Both Pistachio and Rocky Road are favorite ice cream flavors. And Rocky Road is the name of a best-selling candy bar. So a pistachio candy bar ought to sell well, too. It could be called "$TASH" and be designed after the Rocky Road, but contain pistachios instead of cashews. Pistachio nuts are nicknamed "stash" nuts. They are also known to be rather expensive, thus providing the double rationale for the name. Advertising could play up the premium quality of the candy, with one panicky person asking another, "Hey! Have you taken my $TASH?"

√ **Create a souvenir.** What landmarks or natural wonders are closely identified with your locality? Design a product around one of them. Someone sold small pieces of the Golden Gate Bridge cable when it was repaired. San Francisco sourdough bread is shipped all over the country.

Go to the nearest airport and study the souvenirs. San Francisco Fog is sold in a can. You can purchase Mount St. Helens ash in Seattle. How about Los Angeles Smog? Salt Lake Salt? An Ounce of Niagara Falls?

√ **Commemorate something.** There are numerous products commemorating specific events—anything from a national holiday to a local footrace. Design a button, a certificate, a list of entrants, a list of winners, a poster, a T-shirt, a replica of an important site, or a replica of an unimportant local site, treated as if it were an international tourist attraction.

Nearly 100,000 runners show up for the San Francisco Bay to Breakers footrace every year, and thousands of them buy official race T-shirts to remind them of their day. Rock concert promoters make a tidy profit from sales of T-shirts specially designed for each show. Frenzied fans pay premium prices for these fashions, which they wear to school the next day and then keep in their permanent collections.

How about a product to commemorate the 100th birthday of the world's most popular drink? Cola was invented in 1886, so it is now a full century old. Could you concoct a "SUPERCOLA" to celebrate this major international event? You could even create another event—a "Global Blackout"—to get publicity for your roll-out by printing the following legend on your labels:

> Cola, the world's favorite beverage, is 100 years old in 1986. This calls for a global celebration, a voluntary world-wide lights-out on United Nations Day.
>
> It will move around the earth by time zone, with no lights from nine p.m. to midnight. Three hours of primeval darkness for everyone on Earth on the same day. All will have the chance to see the full splendor of the night sky. It will be the first time for many. And it will be the first time the whole planet acts as one. Write to The Supercola Company for details.

√ **Reverse a trend.** Consider whether the world is ready for the opposite of a current trend. SUPERCOLA also fits this category. Everything is "light" these days—light beer, light foods, light wine. Why not be out in front when the pendulum swings the other way?

Paul Newman is successfully marketing an "industrial strength" salad dressing. Why not cola? It is the world's favorite beverage. Americans drink fifty percent more soft drinks than milk, and over half of them are cola. SUPERCOLA could be the first "heavy-duty cola" and hark back to the days of the original syrupy, fountain colas: more sugar, more flavor, more fizz, more fun.

√ **Concoct a contest.** Cola is the world's favorite flavor, but it is not even mentioned in most cookbooks. You could ask consumers to send in cooking-with-cola recipes and award prizes for the best ones. What will they send? Cherry cola pie; cola mousse; cola kilo cake; Mexicola sauce; colaque sauce; sweet colatoes; roast porkola; cola granola?

Once you have enough recipes, you can publish and sell SUPERCOLA Cookbooks along with little bottles of cola syrup and cola extract, which rightfully belong next to their vanilla and almond cousins in the kitchen cabinets of the world.

√ **Rent a famous name.** Annual retail sales of licensed goods in the United States are measured in the billions of dollars, and they are constantly increasing. Trade journals for retailers and manufacturers carry ads for companies making licenses available. Celebrities have agents to contact, and large corporations have licensing sales managers. Licensed products often have a relatively short life expectancy of perhaps one to two years. Still, they can be extremely profitable during their popular periods.

Names and likenesses of cartoon characters, sports figures, television and movie stars, and other celebrities can be "rented" for use with approved products. Garfield and Snoopy logos are raining down on everything like cats and dogs.

Lucasfilm licenses Star Wars characters to select customers willing to pay the record fifteen percent royalties. Coca Cola is now licensing its trademark for use on clothes. There are Yves Saint Laurent cigarettes and Levi's car and truck interiors. Oscar de la Renta has rented his name for a collection of Barbie Doll fashions. The possibilities are endless.

√ **Create your own marketable logo.** Instead of licensing someone else's logo, you may be able to develop your own rentable character or brand name. Esprit fashions created an extremely valuable logo. Another company, L. A. Gear, began manufacturing status clothing. Now it has sold most of its production facilities and simply purchases various clothes and accessories for sale under the L. A. Gear name.

Certain small wineries, having established high-priced images with their limited production, purchase bulk wine from larger wineries and bottle it under their own exclusive labels. They buy this wine by the tanker truckful for a buck or two a *gallon,* and sell it as their own for five to ten dollars a *fifth.* That amounts to a twenty-five hundred percent mark-up on the liquid.

√ **Add a theme.** Associate a product with another country or an ethnic group. Swiss chocolate and German cars are popular because they impart certain images. Can you think of any products that could profitably be associated with India, for example? Give a current product a space-age theme or connect it with a historical period or style.

√ **Borrow from the past.** How about using famous names from history? There will be no royalties to pay. You could create a whole line of imaginative items beginning with, say, "Freudian Slips." These would be sexy nighties and negligee with suggestive phrases from the writings of Sigmund Freud.

Printed clothing is popular at present, as is lingerie. "Freudian Slips" could be a hot-selling fad or perhaps develop into a long-lasting business of unique designer fashions, including "Helen of Troy Halters" and "Cleopatra Panties" for women; "Brandeis Briefs" for men, and "da Vinci Diapers" for toddlers.

√ **Tie in with a cause.** Although it may seem exploitative at times, many companies use popular movements in their merchandising and promotions. Products have been developed around causes such as ecology, ending hunger, and efforts for saving endangered species.

As warfare becomes increasingly unthinkable, causes such as survival and world peace will probably become more and more lucrative as entrepreneurs and existing companies go after the billions of dollars currently spent on armaments.

√ **Use popular symbols.** In the sixties and seventies, the peace symbol and the yin-yang logo were popular. The Good Karmal candy bar uses a modified yin-yang design in its label. What are today's symbols? What products could be created around them?

√ **Import something or bring a proven product to a new location.** A product that is "new" simply because it has not yet been seen in an area is still new, and it has the advantage of having already been successfully tested in other locations. Examples include New York delicatessens, Philadelphia cheese steaks, and numerous theme stores.

Products from other countries can be repackaged or restyled for untapped markets back home. The first teas imported to Europe from the Far East made fortunes and built empires. A more recent example of this type of marketing is the toothpaste-in-a-pump, which was invented in Europe and quickly brought to North America.

Another foreign product that was successfully imported to the United States is the selection of inexpensive, brightly-colored, waterproof watches from Switzerland, some of which are perfumed.

√ **Market an industrial strength product for everyone.** Make available to ordinary consumers a product that has traditionally been sold only to industrial users. Pesticides, cleaners, automotive accessories, and furniture are a few good examples.

√ **Sell status.** What things do people purchase primarily for the privilege of showing they own them? Can you create one with more status? What products are prized merely because they are expensive or new? Can you create a better one? A different one? A newer one? How about a line of expensive designer clothing boxes called "The Emperor's New Clothes"? You sell only the empty boxes. No clothes enclosed.

People like to wear their ski lift tickets for days or weeks, sometimes years, after they have returned from the slopes. Why not market packets of used ski lift tickets for anyone to buy and attach to their clothing for that winter sports "in" look?

√ **Do we live in a time whose idea has come?** Perhaps we live in a time whose idea will come *back.* Are there products that failed because they were "ahead of their time"? Has their time come now? Find products that should have made it but didn't. Can you reintroduce them and make them successful with the aid of modern marketing techniques?

The checklists in the preceding chapters are extensive, but they are not exhaustive. Use them as guides to get you going. Then go off on your own. Don't let the lists limit you. Try to come up with concepts that create new categories. Some of the best ideas come from previously unexplored realms. In new product creation and development, the paramount objective is to come up with something *new*.

The next chapter presents idea-generating exercises for you to try in the real world. It is a wonderful feeling, getting ideas. You may search for the limits of your creativity. Left alone, like the Sorcerer's Apprentice, you may even get carried away.

CHAPTER 4:   IDEAS EXERCISES

The *GoochyGoo* Chronicles

This place is amazing! I never realized it before. This store
has everything. If somebody dropped in here from the
seventeenth century, they'd go instantly insane . . . . . Look
at those labels! Look at the names of those products! Fruit
Loops, Lucky Charms, Trix, Kix, Pac Man, Mr. T, Cap'n
Crunch, Cocoa Puffs, Cocoa Pebbles, Cheerios, Count
Chocula, Franken Berry, Fruity Pebbles . . . . . It's endless.
Everything looks so friendly. Every package says, "Pick me
up and take me home." But the competition is fierce. It's
warfare. Every product has so many competing brands. Ha
ha. Except one. Ha ha ha . . . . . I wonder if there are other
products without any competition. Maybe I could develop a
whole line of merchandise. But what do I look for? How do I
find more holes in the market? I'll have to be scientific about
this. Go down every aisle. Examine every package. Take
notes. Maybe go into a trance. Become like a Buddha; that's
how to see what isn't there. It's like that one hand clapping
stuff. I have to learn how to expand my awareness, open my
consciousness to the mysterious vibrations of the Great
American Supermarket . . . . . People will think I'm crazy.
But look at them. They're crazy too. Putting Cap'n Crunch
and Count Chocula into their carts. We are all crazy.
Pushing our carts up and down these aisles. Ramming into

other carts. Ramming into each other . . . . . I can't take any more input. I'll have to come back another day. This is going to take practice . . . . .

Everyone has ideas. But how do you get really good ideas in specific areas? It requires preparation and training. You have to exercise your right brain, train your creative side. Almost anyone can run around the block. But to run a marathon demands discipline and a special kind of training effort. While reading the preceding checklists has no doubt begun to stimulate your imagination, your best ideas will come after some creative conditioning in the real world.

The following exercise series is designed to saturate you with the latest cultural forces and consumer trends so you will be better able to see what is coming next. The series comprises a unique training system for increasing creativity. It is intense. It may overwhelm you. Immerse yourself at your own pace.

It is not necessary to do all the exercises or to do them in the order given. Adapt them. Change them to fit your own interests and objectives. Do those exercises that appeal to you. Repeat them from time to time. While doing them you will spend some money. Think of it as an investment. Or as entertainment. Or both. But don't worry. It is an essential part of the idea-getting process: *A little carefree spending clears the mind for the formation of new ideas.*

Exercise #1—The Yellow Pages Warm-Up

Read the Yellow Pages. Browse through them or read them from cover to cover. Spend as much time as you want. Do this exercise on a weekday, so that businesses and offices will be open to take your calls. If you don't know what something is, call up and ask. Notice how much space is devoted to the various subject categories. Do you know what the longest are? Find out.

This book, which is free and found virtually everywhere, contains fascinating information. If you live in a small community, get the Yellow Pages from the closest large city. Do not skip this interesting and informative warm-up. It is vital preparation for the exercises which follow.

Exercise #2—The Bestseller Blitz

Check your local newspaper or *The New York Times* for the top ten national bestsellers for fiction and nonfiction. Go to a bookstore and read the first and last chapters of each of these books. You can read more if you want, but you don't have to. And you don't have to enjoy them or remember anything. Just quickly expose yourself to as much as you can. It is helpful to know what is popular. It is interesting to find out what everybody is reading. Buy any of the books you feel like reading further. If you like this exercise, repeat it about every six months.

Exercise #3—Prime Time Playground

Check with a newspaper or local television station to find out the top ten prime time TV shows. Watch them all the way through, including the commercials, within one week's time. This is what everybody is watching. Pretend you are a sociologist, a trained observer of society and culture. Pay special attention to the advertisements. Ask yourself, "What is being sold? Is it a product or an image? A desire or a need? What are they really saying? What are these songs and jingles telling me to do? What benefit do people get from buying that product? Who else is watching? What are *they* thinking?" Think of other questions to ask yourself about the shows and the commercials. Some of our country's top creative talent is at work here. Repeat this exercise about every six months.

Exercise #4—The Reference Library Rampage

Go to a large library, preferably a good business library. Talk to a librarian and ask for a quick tour of the business reference books. Consider yourself a traveller in a new and strange land with only a few hours to find out as much as possible. The amount and detail of information you will discover here is beyond anything you ever imagined (unless you previously attended business school, of course). You can learn everything from a company's annual income to the names of the schools attended by its chief executive officer. Browse through everything and anything that looks interesting. Don't miss highlights such as:

- *Million Dollar Directory* from Dun & Bradstreet

- *Reference Book of Corporate Managements* from Dun & Bradstreet

- All the *Standard Rate and Data* books for advertising information

- *Thomas Register of American Manufacturers*

- *Standard & Poor's Register of Corporations, Directors and Executives*

- *Encyclopedia of Associations*

- *Standard Directory of Advertisers*

This is only a small sample, and there is a wealth of information in each reference book. You will discover things such as the following:

- A full-page color ad in Playboy Magazine costs about $65,000. One in Newsweek runs about $50,000. Or you can buy a full page in the Wall Street Journal for around $75,000. These are all prices for one insertion. The page in the Wall Street Journal is in black and white, of course.

- General Mills began in 1928 with Wheaties and Betty Crocker Flour. Today it owns the following brands, subject to recent acquisitions and divestitures: Country Corn Flakes, Breakfast Squares, Lucky Charms, Fun Pack, Kix, Nature Valley Granola Bars, Cheerios, Cocoa Puffs, Total, Corn Total, Yoplait yogurt, Crazy Cow, Wheaties, Andy Capp's potato snacks, Franken Berry, Buc Wheats, Kaboom, BooBerry, Frosty's, Fruit Brute, Golden Grahams, Trix, Count Chocula, Gold Medal Flour, Red Band Flour, Slim Jim sausages and beef jerky, Potato Buds, Gold Medal Wondra, La Pina, Complete Pancake Mix, Jesse Jones meats, O-Cel-O sponges, Bac Os imitation bacon bits, Betty Crocker baking mixes and potato casseroles, Bisquick mixes, Tom's snack products, Pioneer Products cake decorations and novelties, Hamburger Helper, Tuna Helper, Mug-O-Lunch, Gorton's frozen seafood, Saluto frozen Italian foods, Pemmican beef jerky, Louise's Home Style Ravioli Company, Penrose pickled meats, Good Earth Restaurants, Red Lobster Inns, Betty Crocker Pie Shops, York Steak Houses, Casa Gallardo, Fennimore's, Hannahan's, LeeWards Creative Crafts hobby supplies, Wallpapers to Go, Kittinger English furniture reproductions, Eddie Bauer sports equipment, Pennsylvania House and Dunbar furniture, Monopoly, Clue, Happy Days, Pay Day, Ouiji, Sorry, Bonkers, Boogle, Nerf, Lionel trains, Craft Master paint-by-number sets, Play-Doh, MPC model kits, Discovery Time preschool toys, Darci Cover Girl, Baby Alive, Easy Bake ovens, Spirograph toys, Give-A-Show projectors, Merlin, Sector, Star Wars toys, The Talbots clothing, David Crystal apparel, Monet costume jewelry, Ciani jewelry, Haymaker, Crystal Sunflowers, Lord Jeff clothing, Ship'n Shore apparel, Foot-Joy golf shoes, Chemise Lacoste, and Izod fashions.

- Cola is the world's best selling product. It is made almost entirely from sweeteners and water. Americans alone spend over $20,000,000,000 each year on soft drinks. More than half of this is for colas.

You will literally have to rampage through the place to cover everything quickly in a morning or afternoon. It is possible to spend days looking through the *Thomas Register* alone. It comprises nineteen volumes. Basically, you just want to scout out the library and see what is there so you will know where to come back for more intense and specific research later.

The importance of the business library for new product creation and development cannot be overemphasized. The shortcut to all its information is the reference librarian. Introduce yourself. He or she will be delighted to help.

Exercise #5—The Magazine Store Mini-Marathon

The Magazine Store Mini-Marathon takes one day. It may be repeated as often as you like. Someday soon, when you have no commitments and nothing planned, go to your area's best magazine store. Look through every periodical that strikes your fancy. Be sure to look at those you have never read before. You will find ones you have never *seen* before and ones you never dreamed existed. Skim or read any that interest you. Scan the titles of articles. Look at everything, especially the ads. Absorb as much new input as possible.

What trends do you notice in coverage? What products have the most ads? Which ones have the best ads? Remember, all of these magazines exist because of the ads. What is on the covers? What are the pictures? The words? Why?

If anything seems especially interesting, buy the magazine. Cars, computers, health, teen romance, science, science fiction, sports, gossip, whatever. This will enable you to read items and articles in detail and use them later in the second half of this exercise. It will also keep the store manager from bothering you for spending so much time browsing.

Take as much time as you need. The only requirements are to look at as many new magazines as possible and buy the ones which have some special appeal for you.

As soon as possible after you get home, go through your magazine purchases and cut out things that intrigue or fascinate or otherwise interest you. Cut these up any way you want. Then arrange them in a permanent collage on heavy paper or cardboard. Glue or tape them together and hang your masterpiece on the wall where you will see it often. Your collage represents your personal condensation and distillation of the millions of dollars and thousands of hours of journalistic, artistic, and merchandising effort that went into producing the publications you bought.

Hanging up your collage serves another function. You are letting the people you live with know what you are up to. It is essential that they know about and, hopefully, support your creative activities. You are serious about your new product endeavors. You will be spending time and money pursuing your project. You must be open with those people who are close to you. Talk with them. Share your inspirations. Let them give you feedback. They can help.

Your collage is now hanging in your home, and your housemates know what you are doing. What now? You looked at dozens of magazines in that store on that date. All of that input is now in your subconscious, and your collage is your reminder. It is a souvenir, like the T-shirt you get at the end of a race. Only it is better. It is a work of art. It will inspire you. It is a profound statement about your world, the world as you see it. And it has gotten you in shape for the next exercise.

Exercise #6—The Mall Marathon

This three-part exercise is a marvelous means of generating new product ideas. Some Saturday soon after your Magazine Store Mini-Marathon, when you have nothing else to do, go to your favorite shopping center. Go alone. And walk.

You are on vacation. This is a big amusement park. A carnival. It's kindergarten for big kids. You're a "grown down" for a day. You are in a strange land. You are an E.T. A visitor from the seventeenth century.

You are not to buy anything. Just walk. And look. Go through as many stores as possible. Check every counter. Every display. Every package. Every brand. Every price. Every everything. Do not try to understand anything. Do not buy anything. Do not try to get ideas. Just walk and look. You are a sponge. Sightsee for around six to eight hours. Absorb.

Return on your next free Saturday. Follow the same program. Only this time pretend you have a camera with a high-quality zoom lens. "Take pictures" of everything that interests you. Individual products. Groups of competing products. Displays. In-store advertising. Labels. Names. Shelf arrangements. Packaging comparisons. Price comparisons. Customers' reactions as they consider or select products. Anything. Everything.

It is possible to do this with a real camera. It takes nerve and might reduce the effectiveness of this exercise if it makes you anxious or self-conscious. People will give you strange looks, and store managers will ask what you are doing. But if you are able to do it, you will get a great collection of slides for home study later.

Whether you take real or mental pictures, take rolls and rolls. Collect your images for a minimum of six hours. During this time you are a famous fashion photographer, a noted photo-journalist, and an artist-philosopher-genius. Your shopping center photos will have great sociological impact. Let your imagination go crazy. No shopping. No drugs. Just get high on creativity. And inspiration. And walking and absorbing. Once again, no ideas. Not this week. Next week.

Next week, the following Saturday, go back to the shopping mall with a pen, a notebook, and lots of cash. Green dollars. Enough so you feel that you have plenty to spend and are going to spend plenty.

Walk through the same old stores for another six to eight hours. You know them pretty well by now. Let the ideas come: product names, advertising concepts, new twists, new combinations of things. Everything you absorbed on the previous two visits will begin emerging from your subconscious. You have prepared the ground for new ideas, and now you are going to let them sprout.

And it is time to notice what you do *not* see on the shelves. What products do not exist that should exist? What existing product has no competition? What would you call a new product to compete with it? What would the package look like? Who would buy it?

Write it all down. Make drawings and sketches of logos and packages for your new product ideas. Draw charts and diagrams. Design labels. Whatever comes. Do not study, analyze, or edit. There will be time for that later. The important thing now is to let it all come up, and write it all down now. Everything. Write it down!

And buy things. Anything you want. Especially things for immediate consumption. Instant and total gratification. Chocolate. A new hat. Ice cream. A present for your mate. A steak sandwich. Gifts for friends and relatives. Do some Christmas shopping for next year. You have plenty of cash. Spend it. Buy whatever you want. Especially buy things for yourself. Play out your every consumer fantasy. Indulge. You are worth it.

When you get loaded down, make a trip to the car. Take a short break. Be sure to buy those things which inspire you, items you want to bring home to study further. Maybe you especially like the name or the packaging. Whatever. It doesn't matter. It's only this once. It's for getting ideas. It's worth it. Remember, a little carefree spending clears the mind for the formation of new ideas.

It's over. You have shopped and written and sketched for several hours. It is now time to cool down after your Mall Marathon. Before you drive home in your car stuffed with products and your head full of input, sit there and take care of any last brainchildren. Keep writing for at least fifteen minutes. It will help to clear your head and prepare you for re-entry into your everyday existence.

Exercise #7—Seige of the Art Supply Store

This exercise will require several hours and another outlay of cash. Go to the best art supply store in the area and examine everything. Talk to sales people. Talk to other customers, other creative geniuses! Take your time and find out how to use all the tools and materials that catch your fancy. Think of your best new product concepts and imagine how they would look, how they would be packaged and displayed, and how they would be advertised. Then buy whatever you think you will need for making the packages, labels, and sample ads for them.

At home, experiment with designs for your best products and packages. They do not have to be perfect at this time. Work on concepts with the most meaning for you and which you believe have the most potential for success.

Exercise #8—Making a Preliminary Prototype

Making a prototype will teach you more about your idea than just about anything else you do. A good working model is also essential for an effective presentation if you hope to sell the concept to a company. This exercise is for making a mock-up, model, or preliminary prototype. More detailed information on prototypes is presented in Chapter 6. If your idea is beyond your technical abilities, you should get help. But for now, do this exercise just to learn what is involved. It will help you know how to handle prototype production later when you are working on your million-dollar project.

Many of the things you purchased in the last two exercises will be of use in making a prototype or mock-up, but you are probably going to need some more specialized items. So it is time to repeat the last exercise in the appropriate store or stores. From your Mall Marathon you now know precisely which stores have what.

If you have an idea for a new brand of skin lotion, you may want to look for the perfect container at the drug or department store. You can buy the one you like best, put your own label on it, fill it with a sample of your own formula, and—presto!—instant prototype.

If your idea is for a better mousetrap, you will want to explore the materials at the hardware store. If it is an idea for a new food product, go to the grocery store to buy supplies and to re-examine the competition.

Say you want to make "coffee bags." You think that instant and freeze-dried coffees leave much to be desired. You have an idea for putting fresh coffee in individual filter bags so that it is as easy to make a cup of real coffee as it is to make a cup of tea. You buy fresh-ground coffee, tea bags which you will empty and fill with the coffee, and anything else you might need. Experiment. Does it work? How does it taste? Try it on others. Maybe you need a different filter paper. Will the individual bags need to be vacuum-packed in cellophane to preserve freshness? Call an expert. Design the package. What's the name? "Real Bean Bags?" What's the advertising slogan? "Easy like tea, good like coffee!"

Or, possibly, your top idea is for a new line of automobile hood ornaments. You have noticed that many new cars do not have them. And you have learned at the auto parts store in the mall that no one is making and selling novel and contemporary hood ornaments. You think a line of dinosaurs, teddy bears, and sharks would sell well.

Now you check auto supply and other stores to make certain that such items are not already on the market. Then you go to the toy stores to purchase the things that you want to use for models. At this point you have what you need to prepare prototypes, packaging, advertisements, and so on. You can put together a preliminary presentation to show to trusted friends or associates in order to get valuable feedback on whether to proceed further with this idea.

Exercise #9—The Single Product Brainstorm

Select an existing product of any sort, perhaps one you saw advertised on the Prime Time Playground or something that especially caught your fancy at the mall. Or choose any ordinary product that you have around the house. Put it or a picture of it in front of you at your desk. Make a list of all its features and characteristics, including not only physical properties and functions, but also intangible, psychological, and social ones. List everything you can think of.

Next consider all the ways each of those characteristics could be changed, just for the sake of change. Can any of them be emphasized, exaggerated, reduced, deleted, duplicated, or otherwise altered?

Think of changes to individual features and to the entire product. Take it apart; turn it upside down, inside out; alter its size or the size of a part; rearrange it; rename it; remove part of

71

it; change its form; break it into two or more products; change its container; add something, such as color, scent, decoration, or ingredients; combine some of its parts with another product; add a time element; change the timing by making it function faster or slower.

Observe where you end up. Do any of these alterations or combinations of changes have special merit or suggest any additional new product ideas?

Now make a list of everything that is wrong with "your" product, no matter how seemingly insignificant. Again, think of social and psychological aspects as well as physical ones. Now brainstorm ways to overcome those shortcomings.

Look again at your list of attributes. Can any of them be applied to another product, one totally unrelated to the first? Take a hard look at that other product. Can you see any relationship between it and the first one?

What are the major competitors of the product you are brainstorming? Place them or pictures of them next to the original. What are the differences in price, quality, packaging, and advertising? How would you make "your" product better than the competition? How could you convince consumers of its superiority? How do you like thinking about these things?

Together with the checklists, these exercises should help you find new product concepts without much difficulty. If you want additional sources of ideas, they are readily available, as seen in the next chapter.

CHAPTER 5: OUTSIDE SOURCES FOR NEW PRODUCT IDEAS

The Goochy Goo *Chronicles*

Easy boy. Easy. Slow down. Don't want to get a ticket. Better not get carried away . . . . . I'll have to check the trade journals. See what's happening in the cosmetics and household products industries. Also better pay a visit to the Small Business Administration. Check out all the good old government regulations. But I'll bet anything that there won't be any testing requirements or FDA registration nonsense. In fact, I remember hearing that the guy who invented Vaseline used to eat the stuff. Hmmm, "Petroleum jelly, the natural grease, keeps the doctor away for weeks and weeks" . . . . . It's the perfect product. I can't wait 'til tomorrow morning. I'll make twenty-seven million phone calls, research Goochy Goo in one day. I have to put it on the market before someone else gets the idea . . . . . Easy boy. Whoa. Don't get paranoid, guy. Just get home. Fix the sink and wait 'til tomorrow. Relax. Watch TV. Meditate. . . . . . ♪♪♪ Thank heaven for Goochy Goo . . . . . ♪♪♪♫♪

New product ideas do not have to come solely from your imagination. Many are contained in easily accessible sources, fully developed and available to anyone who wants them. In addition, there are numerous and diverse outside sources to help find and fathom current and coming trends and to use as starting points for creative thinking.

Trade Journals

Trade journals exist for every type of business. There are hundreds of them, including everything from *American Christmas Tree Journal* to *Milk and Liquid Food Transporter*. They are the most important sources of information for the latest manufacturing and merchandising developments in particular industries. They also provide the best detailed data on new products and consumer demand for goods and services.

All industries have trade magazines, but you have probably never heard of most of them. They are usually not available to the general public. They are not sold on magazine racks, and only a few are found in most libraries. Nevertheless, it is easy to obtain sample copies by simply writing and asking for them. Trade journals are issued by business and industry associations or by independent publishing houses. You can find names and addresses in *National Trade and Professional Associations of the United States, Writer's Market*, and various indices to periodicals, all available at the library. You will also usually find the relevant trade magazines in the reception areas of distributors' and manufacturers' offices.

Many of these journals are distributed free, as advertising pays production costs, and trade members are eager to have new potential buyers as readers. You may receive most of them just by sending in their ubiquitous blow-in and rip-out complimentary subscription cards. Some require you to be in the trade. Don't worry, as a "new product developer" you qualify.

Two very special trade journals are *Advertising Age* and *Adweek*, both of which *are* for sale on some magazine racks. These are the gossip sheets and in-depth news services of the advertising industry. They are must reading for anyone interested in new product development. If you have never read these magazines, do so. Among other things, they will tell you how much certain companies are spending on specific ad campaigns, who is stealing whose accounts, and how agency X plans to get the public to buy product Y, made by company Z. The ads themselves, most of which are sophisticated and polished plugs for media in search of advertising dollars, are thoroughly fascinating.

Reading trade journals will stimulate your thinking and keep you abreast of current and coming trends, products, and technologies. Look for parallel developments in different businesses and industries. These are the clues to the big breakthroughs. Exploring the forces which cut across and overlap one or more areas will stretch your mind and make room for more and better concepts.

Newsletters

There are thousands of newsletters published on every topic imaginable. While some consist mainly of jargon and recycled nonsense, many are genuinely informative and useful. Several that deal specifically with new products are: *New Product News,* an ad agency monthly geared mainly to consumer products (Dancer Fitzgerald Sample, 405 Lexington Avenue, New York, NY 10174); *New Product—New Business Digest,* a monthly General Electric Company publication listing its available patents (GE, 120 Erie Boulevard, Schenectady, NY 12345); and the *International New Product Newsletter,* a monthly report covering many categories, with emphasis on foreign inventions (6 St. James Avenue, Boston, MA 02116).

Similar newsletters surely exist for areas that interest you. The best sources for locating them are in the library: Try the *Oxbridge Directory of Newsletters,* the *Ayer Directory of Publications,* the *Standard Periodical Directory*, and the *Newsletter Yearbook Directory.* Looking up specific categories, or simply browsing through these directories, is educational and engrossing.

It is a good idea not to subscribe to a newsletter until after you have seen a sample issue, which will usually be provided free upon request. Shopping for newsletters is easy. Take a box of envelopes to the library and address them as you look through the directories. Do a few or a few dozen depending on how curious you are. When you return from the library, make the necessary number of copies of a short letter asking for subscription information and a sample issue. Then stuff and mail the addressed envelopes, and soon you will begin receiving the materials you requested.

Newsletters have a tendency to come and go, so it is advisable not to pay in advance for an extended period.

Trade Shows and Conventions

Trade shows and conventions are especially valuable for anyone interested in new products. They provide a fast and fun way of finding out what is going on in a specific field. These shows and conventions are basically big bashes and little parties thrown by industries, business groups, professional associations, and assorted other organizations and outfits of all kinds. Almost everyone is from out of town and on an expense account. The excitement and party spirit are contagious and make these events especially good hunting grounds for generating ideas and making contacts. Look at everything and load up on literature and business cards as you walk the aisles.

The booths and exhibits range from the simple, two-hundred-dollar, home-made card-table specials of the little entrepreneurs to big corporations' spectacular "environments," which may cost hundreds of thousands of dollars. There always seem to be a few things that create a stir. You can tell what will soon be making it big just by watching the action at the various booths. Exhibitors display their current goods and services, both new and old, and take orders from retailers, wholesalers, and other industry buyers. Very little actual merchandise changes hands, except on the last day, when floor samples are often sold at a discount rather than shipped back to companies' warehouses.

Most industries have large annual trade shows held in a different city each year and lasting for a few days. Some also have smaller regional shows throughout the year. To locate them, consult the trade journals, Gale Research's *Trade Shows and Professional Exhibits Directory,* or *Successful Meetings Magazine's* semi-annual *Exhibits Schedule,* a complete directory of all types of trade shows, organized by industry, date, and city, with contact people and anticipated attendance.

Virtually all major American cities have convention complexes today. For shows close to home, contact the Chamber of Commerce or the state or local government offices in charge of promoting industry and economic development. For information on larger shows, call or write the convention center of any sizable city, and it will send you the current schedule. There will be more events than you ever imagined. A recent schedule for the San Francisco Convention Facilities included the following:

Fiber Optics Communication	West Coast Computer Faire
Knowledge Industry Publications	Natl. Auto. Dealers Assn.
National Fashion and Boutique Show	Winter Gift Show
Intl. Exposition for Food Processors	Produce Marketing Assn.
Communications Workers of America	Women's Faire
Health Industry Distributors Assn.	Mary Kay Cosmetics
Promotional Merchandise Show	Whole Life Expo
Pentecostal Assemblies of the World	American Dental Assn.
American Society of Anesthesiologists	Tennis Industry Natl. Show
Fitness and Health Promotion Show	American Booksellers Assn.
American Home Sewing Assn.	Automotive Market Research
National Hardware Convention	Natl. Automotive Parts Assn.
American Society of Travel Agents	Assoc. General Contractors
National Welding Supply Assn.	West Coast Beauty Supply
Church of Christ Crusade for Christ	Independent Living Expo
San Francisco Automobile Show	Byte Computer Show
Communications Trade Show	Living Sober
International Gourmet Products Show	Computer Showcase Expo
Ford National Heavy Truck Exhibit	Pacific Coast Builders
American Geophysical Union	International Boat Show
Boat, RV and Recreation Show	Antiques Show and Sale
American Institute of Architects	Building Marts of America

Most trade shows and conventions are not of interest to the general public and are therefore not widely publicized. Some are specifically "for the trade," which means they are not open to the public. But that does not mean you cannot get in.

You may gain admission to just about any trade show by establishing your credentials as an exhibitor, buyer, member of the press, or special something or other. You can usually do this by filling out one of the simple registration forms found on tables in the entrance lobby and presenting it at one of many registration booths, along with a business card and, if necessary, a plausible explanation of why you belong there. If the clerk at the first booth won't type up your badge for one reason or another, simply try again at another booth, this time with a smile, a friendly hello, and, perhaps, a different "plausible explanation."

The name badges are different for buyers, exhibitors, the press, and so on. You may want to register as a "buyer" and be sure of a friendly reception at every booth. Sometime try attending a show as a member of the "press" if you want to receive really special treatment. Or get an "exhibitor" badge if you want to be left alone. Whatever you decide to be, you will need a badge to get in. You need not register in advance.

Periodicals

It is imperative to read several magazines and newspapers regularly in order to keep in touch with trends and changes in the marketplace and with what is going on in the world in general. Several periodicals have annual or semi-annual surveys on new products. *U.S. News & World Report* has such a survey twice a year, in the spring and fall. *Fortune* often carries a "products of the year" feature in its December issue. *Better Homes and Gardens* carries articles on new products for the home once or twice a year. Others, such as *Entrepreneur, Popular Mechanics, Popular Science,* and most of the automobile, health, sports, and computer and electronics magazines feature monthly new products sections. *Advertising Age* carries an excellent new products column for consumer products in each issue.

Clip out and file articles you find especially interesting or likely to provoke new product ideas. Occasionally, shuffle these clippings around on your desk to see associations, overlaps, connections, or anything else that arises. You may discover how to apply a breakthrough in one industry or product category to another. Always be open to serendipity, the discovery of valuable things accidentally or unexpectedly. Perhaps you will want to make another collage. Let your mind roam. Write your ideas down. Keep them organized in a conventional or computer filing system.

A good way to find articles on new products is to look under headings such as "new," "new products," or "new product planning," in the various guides to periodical literature at the library. Do not limit yourself to current issues. Old magazines may contain ideas for products that were only "dream machines" decades ago because the technology did not exist to make them at a reasonable cost, or at all. Perhaps you will find an abandoned fantasy that can now be manufactured into a unique new product.

Catalogs

There are hundreds of catalogs. You can find one or more for every conceivable category of goods and services. There are even catalogs of catalogs. They usually have excellent illustrations and descriptions of the latest merchandise. Collect catalogs for product categories in which you are interested. Read catalogs for other areas to expand your knowledge of what is happening in the market in general. Again, clip out pictures of products that interest you. Look for possible combinations of products from the same or different categories.

How-to Books

Buy a simple how-to book that will introduce you to an entire subject matter. The overview you get will stimulate your thought processes without getting you bogged down in the fine points that would interest a serious practitioner. Try to think of products that would be useful in the field. What questions do you have? What difficulties do you encounter? Could they be remedied? How could tools be improved?

You may want to pick a topic about which you know nothing. If you are a klutz with tools, read a guide to building patios and decks. Lack of familiarity can often be an asset for locating obvious needs that the professional overlooks.

Classified Ads

Another good source of new product ideas is the classifieds. Check newspapers, magazines, and newsletters, particularly under the "business opportunities" heading. As with all these sources, the purpose of reading about what other people are doing is not to copy them, but to seed clouds for precipitating your own brainstorms. You can choose the time and intensity of your creative cloudbursts. You may have a gentle downpour of novel notions or a spectacular electrical storm with great flashes of inspired wisdom.

Say you saw an ad for a telescoping stick for toasting marshmallows. While you believe demand for this can't be great, it starts you thinking about other "long-arm" tools. You remember seeing a portable pole for reaching items on high shelves. What about a collapsible tool for turning television controls for those deprived souls without remote? Maybe you could call it "The Magic Wand."

People

As an experiment, tell the people you talk to over a three-day period that you have been trying to think of a new product idea and ask whether they have any they will share. Just about everybody has at least one. Do not be satisfied with their first answer. Ask them what else they have thought of, no matter how silly or seemingly impractical. Also ask them what they wish someone would invent.

Ask people at school reunions, clubs, and business meetings to share their concepts. Cultivate acquaintances in specialized fields and ask them what improvements would be desirable in their areas of expertise. While you are at it, ask what new products they would like to see for home, for recreation, or for anywhere. Keep a list. Edit it later.

Be careful not to betray any confidences. You are not looking for ideas to misappropriate. Rather, you want to stimulate your thinking and learn consumers' needs. And, who knows, by sharing ideas, you may even find a partner.

Meeting others interested in creating and developing ideas is especially inspiring and can stimulate your thinking, even if they will not divulge anything more than a few meaningless hints about their own projects. Career inventors and new product developers tend not to be joiners of groups, and they may be unusually suspicious about the motives of curious people. Nevertheless, inventors clubs, some with annual exhibitions, crop up from time to time. But, because these individuals tend to be too independent to belong to formal associations for very long, they are sometimes short-lived affairs. A few of the more well-established organizations are listed in the Resource Guide.

Manufacturers

Manufacturers sometimes have obsolete dies, tooling, or prototypes they are willing to sell cheap. You can purchase them for "new" product development or adaptation, or simply to inspire ideas. Plastics manufacturers can be especially good sources of obsolete or never-used molds and tooling. A foam rubber football with grooves for easily throwing spirals was developed from an abandoned foundry mold by a California entrepreneur. The unique new ball is called "Zwirl—The Original Screwball." Will it be the next Frisbee?

Computer Databases

New computer databases are created all the time. They can give information that provides starting points for creative thinking. If you have access to a computer, consult a database directory such as the *Omni Databases Directory.*

Government Sources

Many agencies of our federal and state governments carry out excellent research, publish thorough reports and documents, and provide valuable technical assistance and numerous other services of great potential benefit to inventors and entrepreneurs. The cost is usually nominal.

Unfortunately, almost no one knows about these publications and services. For whatever reasons, they are not marketed very well by the government, and you often must do some digging to unearth them. Government addresses change. You sometimes find that the publication you want will not be available for sixty to ninety days, if at all. You will be asked to reorder in two or three months, and, if you do, the publication may still not be in print. Some agencies are definitely more professional and well organized than others.

Although the process of trying to locate and obtain government publications can be excruciatingly frustrating, it is often worth it. Try alternative sources. Write both the originating agency and the Superintendent of Documents, which is the overall government bookseller.

In addition, try visiting one of the many Government Printing Office Book Stores located around the country. They have many of the more popular publications in stock or can order them for you. The many local libraries designated as Depository Libraries have copies of government materials. Write the Superintendent of Documents for a list of their locations.

Finally, try telephoning first to find out if a publication or service is current. When you call, you will often be put on hold, so have some work in front of you to keep you from pulling your hair out while waiting.

Improved promotion and merchandising of these high-quality goods and services are sorely needed. In fact, that just might be a great idea! Federal publications are not copyrighted. Some entrepreneur will surely start to copy and sell them on a grand scale, probably making a fortune in the process. In the meantime, the following paragraphs highlight the current government publications and services most helpful for new product development. A more complete listing is found in the Resource Guide.

The addresses for these and other resources are mentioned in the text to encourage you to write immediately for the publications that interest you. Act now. If you put off writing, there is a good chance you never will get around to it. Keep some paper and a box of envelopes nearby and address them as you read.

- *Superintendent of Documents, Government Printing Office, Washington, D.C. 20402.*

This is the bookseller for the United States government. There are publications on an extensive variety of topics, including current research, business, energy, space, health, gardening, home economics, children, and many more. Reading through these can help trigger ideas.

Catalogs and price lists are available free of charge. *Price List 36* contains periodicals listed by government agency and by subject, including business, population, economic indicators, waste, and many others.

The *Subject Bibliography Index* lists bibliographies of government publications by topics. Order them for subject areas that interest you, and then order individual publications from them.

New Books is a bimonthly catalog of new releases by subject matter. A free subscription is available on request.

- *National Technical Information Service ("NTIS"), and Center for the Utilization of Federal Technology, 5285 Port Royal Rd, Springfield, VA 22161.*

NTIS is probably the single most important government resource for anyone interested in new product development. It provides current information in a vast number of subject areas. Write for all this agency's literature and review it carefully.

NTIS is the central clearinghouse for public sale of government-sponsored research and development, and it maintains reports on foreign technology and market data. It is also in charge of licensing federally patented inventions for commercial use.

Some of NTIS's two million titles are listed in *General Catalog of Information Services; Public Searches Master Catalog; Foreign Technology Abstract Newsletter; Foreign Technology Catalog; Catalog of Government Patents; Government Inventions for Licensing;* and the *Directory of Federal Technology Resources.*

There are also periodicals in a number of subject areas, including computers, manufacturing, testing, machinery, energy, and instrumentation. The annual *Federal Technology Catalog* accompanies most subscriptions.

An especially relevant service is the monthly *Tech Notes*, illustrated fact sheets of new processes, equipment, software, materials, and techniques developed by federal agencies and considered to have practical or commercial potential. An annual catalog is available. *Weekly Abstract Newsletters* summarize newly released research and development reports.

Through NTIS's standing order microfiche service, called "SRIM," you can automatically receive documents within any specified category as they become available.

NTIS is in charge of federally generated computer data files and software. It offers customized searches of research data. *Bibliographic Databases* contains the latest technical reports on already completed research. Bibliographies of past searches in certain specified areas can be found in *Published Searches*. In addition, the *Federal Research in Progress Database* contains some seventy thousand on-going research projects.

- *Department of Commerce, Washington, D. C. 20234*

Various divisions of the Department of Commerce are helpful in the new product field. Especially useful are the Business and Defense Services Administration and the National Bureau of Standards. Write for full information about their services and publications.

The Clearinghouse for Federal Scientific and Technical Information, Springfield, VA 22151, will send information on trends in specific industries and new scientific fields, technical reports, marketing data, and new product information. Be sure to request the *Business Services Bulletins* and the *Distribution Data Guide*, both of which provide information on various types of products and services.

The National Inventors Council and the Office of Technical Services of the Department of Commerce no longer exist.

- *Patent and Trademark Office, Washington, D.C. 20231*

The *Official Gazette* is the journal of the Patent and Trademark Office. It lists and summarizes patents granted each week and some that are available for sale or license. Reading about these patented concepts will inspire your own creative thought. Write the Patent and Trademark Office for information and request the complete list of other publications relating to patents, trademarks, inventions, and new products.

Of special interest are the following: *Patents and Inventions: An Informal Aid for Inventors; Questions and Answers About Patents; The Disclosure Document Program; General Information Concerning Patents; Patents and Government Developed Inventions; Technology Assessment and Forecast;* and *Patent Profiles.*

Copies of individual patents are available for $1 each. Delivery takes three to four weeks.

Look around the stores for products similar to yours or which might be useful for design purposes. If patented, the item or package should bear the patent number. Order a copy. Reviewing it will demonstrate how it works and help you analyze whether your idea would infringe it.

* *Small Business Administration ("SBA"), Post Office Box 30, Denver, Colorado 80201-0030; toll-free SBA referral number: (800) 368-5855.*

The most useful SBA publications are *Ideas into Dollars; Decision Points in Developing New Products; Basic Businesss Reference Sources; Can You Make Money with Your Idea or Invention?; New Product Development; Introduction to Patents;* and *New Product Ideas.* Also request the catalogs for Management Assistance Publications.

The *Monthly Products List Circular,* which lists inventions for license or sale, is of interest.

See the Resource Guide for additional federal resources. Also start finding out about your local and state agencies' publications and programs by calling appropriate listings found in the telephone book. Remember, these resources are poorly promoted, but with a little determined investigation, you will discover invaluable treasures. After all, your taxes paid for them so you might as well use them.

In sum, government publications can be invaluable for identifying current trends, new products under development, and concerns of industry, government, and interest groups. Use them as you would any other source of new product ideas—as runways for takeoff on your own creative flights.

Now you know how to get ideas. At this point, you may even have notebooks and tapes of all kinds of concepts. Which ones do you develop? What are the criteria? How do you decide? A comprehensive set of guidelines for screening and evaluating ideas is presented in the next chapter.

CHAPTER 6:   EVALUATING IDEAS

The *Goochy Goo* *Chronicles*

Monday morning. At last. I can begin making calls . . . . .
Good old Yellow Pages . . . . . Let's see, oil companies . . . .
"That's correct, prices for white petroleum jelly . You say you
can deliver in fifty gallon drums for about $220 each? Thank
you. I'll get back to you." Holy cow! That works out to less
than four cents per ounce. And Vaseline sells a one-ounce tube
for $1.79. What a mark-up! . . . . . "Hello, is this White
Pharmaceutical Manufacturers? I want to know how much it
will cost to have you pack some Vasel—, I mean, petrolatum.
One-ounce tubes. Good. Please mail me those quotes". . . . .
Dum de dum. Dum de . . . . . "Is this the reference librarian?
Could you look up how much Americans spent on Vaseline
Petroleum Jelly last year? Yes, total sales". . . . . Dum de
dum. Dum de dum dum duuummm . . . . . "WHAT? FIFTY
MILLION DOLLARS?! That's just for the petrolatum? It
doesn't include all the Intensive Care brands? Good grief!
Thank you, ma'am. Thank you very much". . . . . Man! I
have to shift into high gear. Sure never felt like this on a
Monday morning before . . . . . . Uh oh, I'm two hours late
for work. So what? This is much more important. I'm not
going to work. I'm going to get rich. Get free. Going to be
the next petrolatum mega-mogul of the free enterprise system
. . . . . ♩♩ Goochy Goo is coming down the track. Dum de
dum dum dum . . . . . ♩♩♩♪♬♪

Now that you can have ideas on command, how do you choose one to develop? And how do you objectively evaluate its potential? To answer these questions, begin by asking what you care about. Unless a concept intrigues and excites you, why bother?

Of course, interest and meaning are not the only criteria. You must make a thorough evaluation of your product's profit potential and overall chances for success. Your hunches and intuition need to be tempered with as much careful research as you can do or buy. But even with the most intense and elaborate analysis and testing, you may still be wrong. And you are not alone. Although big companies spend millions on market research, they regularly fall flat on their corporate faces.

In order to profit from an idea, you have to make it more than "just an idea." This is true even if your only goal is to sell the concept rather than to develop it yourself. When a company buys an idea, it is also buying your preparation and presentation. It wants to be sure that the concept can be made into a real product at a reasonable cost and that people will buy it. The company will make its own analysis and judgment, of course, but unless you present your well-thought-out conclusions on these topics, you may not enjoy an enthusiastic reception. There are certain things you must do. These include finding out if the product has already been done, making a prototype, checking the technical feasibility, calculating costs, estimating a price range, considering legal aspects, and analyzing the potential market.

This chapter constitutes a practical guide for evaluating and screening new product ideas. It covers the following topics:

• Has it been done?

• Technical feasibility and making a preliminary prototype

• Market research and testing

• Consumer acceptance: What makes a new product successful?

- Financial feasibility

- Competitive status

- Distribution

- Preliminary promotional considerations

- Maintenance and service requirements

- Legal, safety, and environmental factors

- Staying flexible and revising your ideas

- Invention marketing services

- Government and university resources

- Appreciating failure and learning from mistakes

Use these guidelines. Modify them. Ignore them when necessary. By all means, add to them. There are very few hard and fast rules for new product development. There is nothing to prevent you from creating and carrying out your own novel analysis. In any event, your evaluations and research activities at this stage are only preliminary. As your product develops, constantly refine and perfect them.

The methods for new product creation and development are intrinsically amorphous and incomplete. When in doubt, make up your own rules. Your goal is to explore unknown realms and discover things unique and different.

Has It Been Done?

To avoid wasting time and money on a project not worth pursuing, you must search the existing market right away. Take your idea for "The Magic Wand," the telescoping rod with moveable hard rubber fingers on the end for manually-operated remote control of the TV. No batteries to wear out. No delicate and complex electronic gadgetry to break down and require costly repairs. You spend a few weeks working on the idea, making a prototype, and playing with packaging ideas and marketing strategies.

Finally, you remember to check the market to see if it already exists. Before you have the chance, you open a novelty catalog that just arrived in the mail, and on the first page, there is a magic wand. Just released. Almost exactly as you had envisioned. It is called the "User Friendly Remote." Your name is better, but what's the difference? You could go ahead and make an improved version and try to enter the market, but you decide that competing for the relatively low profits on this type of product is not appealing. You would prefer to work on something else. Your initial efforts were wasted.

Fortunately, this mistake was not too costly, and it taught you an invaluable lesson: *The first, most important step is to find out if your idea has been done.* As simple as this sounds, people often get so caught up in the excitement of a new concept that they forget it. The fact that you don't remember seeing the product on the shelves is not enough. This step requires thorough research.

If the item is the type that might be patentable, now is the time to do a preliminary search. This is not so much to help you get a patent, but to determine if anyone else already has one. There is no point developing an idea only to discover at the last minute that it would infringe someone else's rights.

Although it is usually not advisable to do your own patent work, a preliminary search at this stage might be one exception. Actually looking at existing patents can be fascinating and instructive. It can help you finalize the design of your product so it does not infringe others' rights. It may also trigger other thoughts and concepts.

If your product idea depends upon use of a particular name, you should investigate whether it is trademarked or otherwise belongs exclusively to anyone else. See Chapter 8 for information on preliminary patent and trademark searches. Finding an existing trademark or patent means you will have to change your concept or make plans for licensing the rights.

There are other essential methods for finding out if your idea has been done. Look in the stores. Read back issues of the relevant trade journals, looking at both articles and ads. Check the classifieds. Look for anything close to your concept. If you find something, follow up. Investigate all clues.

Call manufacturers, wholesalers, and retailers of similar items. Generally describe your product concept and ask if they stock it or have ever seen anything like it. Find out what other products serve similar functions. You can do all this without giving away any secrets. If you have an idea for an underwater field guide for snorkelers, for example, call dive shops. Tell them you are going to Hawaii next month and have heard of a waterproof gismo that helps divers identify undersea life. If they tell you they have a four-by-six plastic card that sells for $3.99, you know you weren't the first to think of the concept.

Trade magazine editors and writers are knowledgeable in their fields and may be contacted for information. Be warned, however, that none of these people has any obligation of confidentiality. Be careful not to give your ideas away.

Even if your concept *has* already been done, that is not necessarily the end of your endeavor. Study the existing product. Buy one of the snorkeling cards. Is your idea significantly different, better, or more appealing in some way? Can it be made so? Is your field guide in a format other than a card? Does it have some means of attaching to the body so it won't float away? Is there a book to go along with it for more in-depth reading on shore?

Perhaps there is room in the market for both products. Could you avoid the competition by aiming at a different target group or using another means of distribution? Most snorkelers are not experienced scuba divers, and they might be more likely to find your product in the travel or nature section of a book store than in a dive shop. Call a few book stores to see if it already exists.

If you find the product has been done, but it failed, study why. If possible, talk with those who made or sold it. See if anything was written about it in periodicals. Perhaps the time was simply not right. Maybe you can think of a different angle or format to make it succeed.

In any case, knowing whether the concept has been done is the first step in your evaluation. It can keep you from wasting time, energy, and money. The second step is to learn whether your great idea can, in fact, be made.

Technical Feasibility and Making a Preliminary Prototype

Reducing your idea to a model or working prototype is critical. It proves that the concept is workable and helps you make improvements in function or design that you might never have known were necessary. It is far better and cheaper to find out about glitches and miscalculations while making one sample of the product rather than after having geared up to make several thousand of them.

If you are going to try to sell the idea, having a prototype is almost a necessity. Most mid-size and larger firms are not interested in hearing about, much less developing, new product concepts which come from external sources. If they do accept an outside idea, it is because, based on hard evidence, including a good prototype, it represents a demonstrably practical and potentially profitable product.

Having a prototype will also aid in market research and in defining your target group of consumers. It is much easier and more reliable to determine people's reactions to a product when you can show them an actual sample, rather than just describing it to them. You can find out their opinions of specific features and why they would or would not buy it.

Making the prototype will also help you begin to analyze the costs involved in manufacturing the product. You can start to determine whether it can be sold at a price which will provide adequate volume for keeping costs low, and, in turn, enough revenue to yield an acceptable profit. If not, you can consider redesign, use of different materials, and other changes that might reduce the costs.

Finally, creating a model gives you the concrete feeling that you are making a commitment. It tests your determination. Making the prototype is the fun and easy part. If you are not willing to spend the time, money, and energy necessary to produce one sample, you had better reconsider how eager and able you are to expend much more time, money, and energy on developing or selling the idea.

At this stage, the prototype will be preliminary. As the product passes through the evaluative screens, refine it and, eventually, make a final version.

Types of Prototypes

How would you go about making a prototype for the one-arm bandage dispenser? You could just reproduce a picture or drawing of a slot machine with a bandage coming out of the jackpot opening at the bottom. Or you could make a full-scale working model. The former would take only a few minutes and cost only a few dollars. The latter could take months to design and make, and it would probably cost thousands of dollars.

The type of prototype you need will depend quite a bit on the nature of your product. If you have designed a new bulldozer, you may not be able to present a fullblown working model due to the size and expense of tooling up for production. But you may be able to produce a functional model of its important points. In every case, your final goal should be to come as close as possible to making a functioning prototype that demonstrates every feature of the product.

- A *production model* is one that is exactly like the final product, using the same materials, sizes, colors, and manufacturing processes. If an order were received, the product could be manufactured in quantity. Of course, the concept can later be changed to incorporate any alterations and refinements.

- A *preproduction model* is made with the type of tooling that will be used in production, but it may differ in some minor respects from the final product. Some adjustments may be contemplated before production begins.

- A *working model,* on the other hand, is made of different materials than those planned for final production. Nevertheless, it is fully functional and strong enough to withstand repeated demonstration and handling. With any functional prototype, the features can—and should—be illustrated through demonstration, rather than mere verbal explanation.

* *Nonfunctioning models* or *mock-ups* are primarily used to show color, shape, size, styling, and design in three-dimensional form. A mock-up may be quite satisfactory for photographs and other preproduction promotional purposes if the item is nonmechanical and if the final version can be closely approximated. It may be all you need if your product consists primarily of graphics, like the underwater field guide. But, if the product has critical functional aspects, it is not sufficient to present a mere nonworking model of its styling and appearance.

  Remember, your goal is to approximate and demonstrate the final product. A less-than-attractive working model is almost always preferable to a beautiful, but nonfunctional, mock-up. Established companies are, in fact, used to dealing with unfinished models. If styling and function are equally important in your product, it can be effective to present both a working model and a finished mock-up.

* *Drawings* or *plans*. These are the least acceptable. They neither demonstrate that the concept can actually be built nor present an effective three-dimensional sample to picque the interest of potentional buyers of your idea.

How to Make a Prototype

As with most of the steps in developing an idea, you can make the prototype yourself, or you can pay someone else to make it. The decision will depend on your talent, available time, financial resources, and the nature of the product. If computers and other electronic devices are needed and you have no expertise in these areas, you will have to get help. On the other hand, if the invention is in your technical field, you probably are the best one to make it. Only you can decide.

If assistance is required, there are companies that specialize in making prototypes and models, and you can find them in the Yellow Pages. They are listed under "Product Designers," "Designers—Industrial," and "Inventors." Also, try calling companies making similar products to see if they can direct you to a suitable designer. Ask your friends and people in your network. Local colleges with industrial design classes may have students or instructors who would be interested in assisting. They know many shortcuts to building inexpensive functioning models.

Professional designers can also be very helpful in perfecting appearance and styling. Studies have shown that people prefer products that are well designed and have "nice lines." They also like things that look familiar, although sometimes an unusual look in itself encourages purchases. Professional product designers can be invaluable complements to your own esthetic judgment and abilities. The costs of hiring experts may in the long run be recouped many times over due to their experience and knowledge.

Depending on the product, you may want to design a package as part of the prototype. For any graphics required, you may achieve a professional-looking result yourself. From having done the "Seige of the Art Supply Store" exercise, you are familiar with the wide variety of materials. Buy what you need, and experiment.

Have fun. The more you enjoy the process, the better your prototype and presentation will be. Experiment with press-on letters, colored papers, and the equipment at your local copy shop, especially the machines that allow enlargement and reduction of your lettering and art. Observe others. Ask for help. Almost anything is possible with these amazing copy machines, which are now available on nearly every other street corner. They allow you to use millions of dollars worth of technology for only a few pennies per page.

You will probably be turning out professional-quality work in a very short time. Always remember, you are making labels and packaging for your own ideas. They are worth the best.

You know better than anyone what they should look like. Certainly you and "your" machines can achieve exactly the right look.

If you require illustrations, you can buy "clip art" at any art supply store. These uncopyrighted sheets or books of drawings are available for every conceivable subject. You can copy and use the material any way you want. Professionals use clip art all the time. Maybe this explains why we often see the same images over and over in local, regional, and even national publications.

Another source of practically-free artwork is old books and magazines on which the copyrights have expired and which are, therefore, in the public domain. Finally, students at local art schools may be willing to provide very good original work at modest rates.

In summary, making a prototype is essential. You should make a preliminary one at the outset and refine it as you go. Having a concrete model will solidify your thinking and will help in everything from market research to selling the idea.

At the same time you are making your prototype, you should be investigating the market. Both you and any company you approach for sale of the idea will want all available market data before making a commitment to introduce the product.

Market Research and Testing

A major cause of new product failures is inadequate evaluation of the market. If you believe your product is marketable, you need to confirm your hunch. First, using secondary sources, research and evaluate the size of the potential market in the abstract. Essentially, you want to estimate how big the market could be. Then do some preliminary research in the real world to find out who will buy, why, and at what price.

Secondary Sources

Statistics relevant to market size and characteristics are readily available in most business libraries. The particular sources to use depend on the product. Your first stop should be at the reference librarian's desk. These unsung heroes are invaluable. They delight in helping people use little-known resources and find obscure facts. In addition, they will often do research and answer questions over the telephone.

Gather as much information as you can. If Ground Control is your product, for example, see if you can find out how many people buy computers each year, how many use a mouse, and so on. You may not be able to find every fact and figure you would like. Get what you can, and then analyze the raw data.

Government publications and databases are quite useful, particularly those of the National Technical Information Service. Write for the many pamphlets describing NTIS's available services and information.

Trade journals are also an excellent source of information about their industries. They often keep statistics and publish summaries of various sorts. By writing or calling the editors, you can learn the best places to look for the data you need.

Think creatively about what facts you need and how to use what you learn. The analysis need not be sophisticated, as long as it is accurate and appropriate. Maybe you have invented a covered dish that keeps butter from getting hard after a cold night on the counter. What are the parameters of the market? You live in Montana. Would people in more southern climates have need for such a device? You doubt the temperature gets very cold at night in Florida, but you really aren't sure. You investigate the seasonal temperatures in different regions and come up with an analysis of areas where the butter dish might be useful.

Ideally, you want to invent something for a "buoyant" category—one that is rising and prospering. Say you developed a new way to shoe horses. Even if every blacksmith in the country purchased your revolutionary system, you would not sell very many. The per-unit cost of making only a few would be high, requiring a high price, which would discourage a certain number of potential buyers. You would be unlikely to have much new competition, given the limited market. However, your real competition would be the existing shoeing methods, which are sufficient and require no further capital expenditure.

Computers are the obvious example of a buoyant category. They are constantly changing. People are interested in them. New applications are being found all the time. The market for computer-related products can be expected to grow.

Real World Research

After this preliminary evaluation, you need to take your idea into the real world. Market research can be a trade-off between risking secrecy and gaining valuable information. It is necessary at some point to find out what the intended consumer thinks of your product. You cannot keep your brainchild to yourself forever.

Market research is a vast and complicated subject. There are companies which specialize in this inexact science, and many advertising agencies have market research and testing divisions. Call or write to a few and ask for their brochures describing their services and fee structures. Now is also a good time to meet some advertising people. Ask friends for recommendations or find them in the Yellow Pages. Better still, find some ads you like and talk to the agencies that made them. Request estimates for preliminary market research and testing programs to give you some idea of the costs. Perhaps you can get a tour of their agencies.

Major corporations have entire divisions that do nothing but market research. Testing on that scale is way beyond your capabilities. Don't worry. Your object at this point is to develop preliminary information. You can conduct very effective market research on a small scale. If a company is interested in your idea, it will initiate its own testing on a much broader basis.

First do an informal version of what market researchers call "concept testing." Simply confide your idea to people you trust. Do they like it? For what reasons? What objections do they have to it? Would they buy it? At what price? Would they purchase it for themselves or give it as a gift, or both? Could be made better? How?

Remember that you targeted a certain group as potential buyers of the product. Make certain that the people you question include, but are not limited to, those in the target. You may discover other target groups as you research. Talking to people other than your friends is advisable to avoid a favorable bias.

You can test your concept by interviews or by written questionnaires. Interviews allow you to ask additional questions and to follow up answers, while questionnaires let you get responses from more people in a shorter time period.

If your idea is greeted favorably in this stage, make your prototype and try some "product testing." Show the model to people and let them manipulate it. Ask them questions. Use your friends or properly selected strangers. If you invented a new stapler, you might stop and interview people in front of an office supply store. Ask if they would buy it, why, and at what price. You may also want to take your prototype to trade shows and gauge people's reactions.

Be wary of positive responses to the question, "Would you buy it?" They may only be indications of curiousity or attempts to spare your feelings. Therefore, also ask questions such as: What benefit does it provide? What need does it fill? What do you like or dislike about it? Does it solve a problem? Answers to these questions more reliably predict consumer interest and willingness to buy.

Conversely, negative responses to the would-you-buy question *are* reliable. Therefore, market research is most reliable for predicting failures, not successes. It can help you avoid disasters, but it will not guarantee winners.

Large companies often "test market" a product by introducing it and monitoring sales in a limited geographic area. The results help determine whether to proceed with a large-scale roll-out. It might be possible for you to do something similar in a more limited way. You should be able to find a few retailers who are willing to take a supply of sample products on consignment. Try different types of stores, different packages, and different prices. Compare the results. This can give you invaluable feedback for designing and pricing your product. You could even stand nearby and watch people's reactions or ask them questions. Any information you obtain can become part of a presentation to potential corporate purchasers of your idea.

Big corporations put their concepts through many screens. They have developed various guidelines and rules of thumb for making go/no-go decisions based on market research. According to one system, unless eighty to ninety percent of the concept test responses are positive, the idea is dropped. Likewise, when a prototype is shown, seventy to eighty percent must respond positively for the product to pass to the next screen. Finally, after seeing a finished product in its final package, sixty to seventy percent must express an intention to buy, or, even at this late date, the project may be scrapped.

You should also be continually re-evaluating your concept, changing it, improving it, and testing it. Use the feedback to perfect your product or change your strategy. Be realistic in your evaluations. And be ruthless if you discover, no matter how late, that the concept is not viable. Move on to the next project.

Consumer Acceptance: What Makes a New Product Successful?

What are the critical factors for success of a new product? The textbooks try to answer this question with theories, definitions, models, arguments, charts, and statistics. Although some of this material may merit study, much of it will only confuse you and drain your enthusiasm. Steering clear of texts is advised. In the end you will probably decide that no one really knows the answers. Consumers are unpredictable. What conventional market research principles could have predicted that millions of people would buy plastic tubes to swing around their hips or little stickers to paste on everything? What MBA or Ph.D. could have predicted the first trivia game?

It certainly seems that logic has little to do with creating a successful new product. Someone tried combining an extremely popular flavor—cola—with a very popular dessert—gelatin. Logic predicted a runaway success. Consumers disagreed, and no one really knows why.

The most obvious factors influencing whether a product will be successful include price, status value, packaging, need

100

fulfillment, quality, and uniqueness. But exactly how these elements apply in a given situation is often difficult to predict.

And then there are the less obvious factors. For example, there may be resistance due to some minor detail that can cloud consumers' perception and, in turn, acceptance. Gerber Products failed with "Singles," small portions of food intended for sale to single people. They were packaged in small glass jars, and the association with unappetizing baby food doomed what otherwise might have been a timely, successful venture.

Additionally, if use of the new product would require extensive instructions or drastic changes of behavior, success may require special educational and promotional strategies. Sometimes consumer resistance can be overcome by associating the item with something familiar.

If use involves behavior that is contrary to an ingrained value, special problems arise. Some motorcyclists are slow to adopt helmets because the idea of taking safety precautions conflicts with their daredevil, risk-taking self-images. To have a successful product under such circumstances, it must somehow be made to seem consistent with users' preexisting values. These sorts of subtle considerations are the ones that often get overlooked in the evaluation process.

Perhaps the single most important point to analyze is the benefit to potential consumers. People will buy a product only if it provides them with a perceived benefit. This analysis is not as easy as it may sound. Many people with product ideas erroneously assume that a new feature alone is sufficient benefit. This is far from true, particularly if competing products are already adequately satisfying the need. The new item must be perceived as supplying a benefit not obtainable elsewhere.

Be especially aware of the consumer's point of view. Sometimes a new product will be built around an exciting technological advance. It may be truly revolutionary from an engineer's viewpoint, but meaningless to ordinary people. Unless the technical brilliance translates into convenience, status, lower price, or some other benefit *that is important to potential consumers,* chances of success are slim.

One of the least expensive and most fruitful ways of assessing potential snags is to brainstorm not *whether* the product will fail, but all the different reasons why it *could.*

Then look objectively at each of those possibilities and evaluate ways of reducing the risks.

Financial Feasibility

You must decide whether making and marketing your product is financially feasible. If the total costs of tooling up, manufacturing, shipping, promoting, and selling preclude making an acceptable profit, the concept must be abandoned or changed. Your financial analysis at this early stage will be preliminary and somewhat general. If your idea makes it through evaluation and screening, you will later make detailed cost, price, volume, and profit studies as you focus on the best way to develop it. Keep records of how your calculations were made in order to document your assumptions and methods. Change the figures as new information becomes known.

In brief, it is important at this point to know the approximate "start-up" or "tooling" costs, as well as projected production and operating costs per unit for the going venture. The cost per unit will vary depending upon the quality desired and the quantity manufactured. Up to a certain point, savings are possible due to quantity purchase discounts and manufacturing economies of scale.

Start-Up Costs

Sometimes it simply requires too much money to tool up for production. Say you have an idea for a unique line of women's high heel shoes. Your concept is to have the heel, or "spike," as it's called, be in the shape of a woman's body from the waist down. These leggy spikes would be very shapely and sexy. They could even be standing in their own little high heels.

You believe your idea has fad and craze potential and would sell well to teenagers and young women for a season or two. Upon research with shoe manufacturers, however, you discover that it requires an inordinate amount of tooling up to begin making the shoes in all the necessary sizes and colors.

So even though you might sell a million pairs, the capital needed and the interest on that capital is probably too great to warrant going into production.

This leggy high heel is still a good concept, but it is perhaps best developed in some other format. It would make interesting jewelry, or some kind of miniature charm, or a shoe store window display, or key ring ornaments for a large shoe company to use as promotional items. Remember, there are many ways to develop an idea. If you have a good concept, stay with it until you find the optimal approach.

Production Costs

First, figure the "direct costs" for parts, materials, and labor. Call suppliers and find out prices and quantity discounts. Next, project labor costs. This can be tricky, as you have to estimate the time required for performing the various manufacturing operations. It may be advisable to do some informal time studies for several people at each of these tasks. Plug in the appropriate wages, remembering to include all applicable taxes and fringe benefits, and you will be able to estimate a range of labor costs.

As an alternative to these somewhat tedious calculations, you may consult with "contract manufacturers" to find out anticipated costs for various quantities. These are companies that tool up and make products according to your specifications. They can give you good estimates based solely on their experience. If you give them a job to bid, they will do detailed cost analyses and provide you with firm quotations.

You can find local contract manufacturers in the Yellow Pages. In addition, many trade and business publications will provide you with comprehensive directories of companies in their fields. Do not limit yourself to local firms. Some parts of the country are centers for certain types of manufacturing. The prices they quote can be lower than local producers' estimates even after adding in shipping costs. Get names and addresses from the *Thomas Register* or the other reference sources with which you are now familiar.

Second, calculate "indirect costs" for marketing, shipping, and overhead, which includes rent, utilities, telephone, office supplies, clerical and administrative personnel, and all other costs of doing business. It is often difficult to assign exact figures for these. Use the telephone to get estimates. It is acceptable to employ guesswork here, but be conservative. Most people tend to underestimate indirect costs.

It will not be possible or necessary for you to try to develop complete cost figures for companies that you may approach, but you should make clear in your analysis that you are aware of them. State your assumptions and be conservative. If you are planning to go into business yourself, you will have to pin down everything. Consult one of the many excellent books on how to start a business for advice on estimating the expenses.

Revenues

Looking at costs is only half the story. You must also consider revenues and profits, and this means thinking about price. Pricing is complex, and you should not try to make final decisions at this point. Analyze whether the product can be sold within a price range that will bring sufficient revenues to justify introducing it. If you can only make a few dollars on an intricate piece of machinery, you may decide that the risks of doing business are too high to warrant going into production.

Setting a price range is difficult. The simplest situation is where your product is similar to or replaces one already on the market. Yours will probably have to be sold at about the same price. On the other hand, if an idea is truly new, becomes a status item, or constitutes a significant improvement, people may pay premium prices for it.

Now tie your financial data to your market data to make projections about sales and total revenues. Evaluate the market over the lifetime of the product. The traditional pattern is for an item to start out slowly, build to maximum sales, and then decline. Novelties may take off quickly and be completely dead within six months. Other products, especially those requiring education—like computers—may be slow to start but then sell well for many years. Is yours a product that will wear out and be rebought? How often? Or will people buy one and keep it forever?

Don't hesitate to get assistance if you have questions, are confused, or just don't understand the first thing about costs, prices, and volume. Never try to hide your lack of knowledge or aptitude in an area. Get help from consultants, suppliers, or knowledgeable friends in business. Distributors, sales reps, and other middlemen are especially good sources for opinions on pricing and product life cycles.

Your financial analysis at this stage need only be detailed enough to enable you to evaluate the basic viability of your idea. If it passes through this screen, your analyses should be refined as you develop the concept.

Competitive Status

Check out the competition. Compare your product not only with similar products, but with ones that fulfill similar needs or provide similar benefits. How many competitors are there? What prices are being charged? What are the profits?

What unique benefit or other advantage does your product have? It could be cost, efficiency, novelty, durability, appearance, status, convenience, or many others. Even if there is no present competition, a successful product will usually attract imitators. How difficult is it to go into production? If significant start-up costs are required, "knock-off" artists will be discouraged. Can you get into production quickly and "skim" the early sales with a high price before anyone can catch up? If profits are high, competition will appear quickly. You do not have to be the only one on the market to succeed, but you need plans for dealing with competition as it emerges.

Distribution

Manufacturing is often only a very minor portion of overall new product development. Distribution will probably require much more expense and effort than you originally anticipate. The type you utilize will depend on your product category and volume.

Determine whether the particular industry has an established distribution structure. Talk with retailers. Ask them how the system works and get the names of reliable middlemen. Make it a point to meet distributors at trade shows. Keep their cards for future reference. Trade journals also will provide lists of their names by area. Call them. Discuss standard mark-ups, demand, pricing, and terms. Find out if they would handle a product such as yours. Ask for their recommendations on how you might improve your idea.

You should be familiar with various types of middlemen:

- *Full-function wholesalers* or *distributors* offer the most complete services. They actually buy merchandise and resell it at a price marked up by a standard percentage. They often sell to a wide variety of retailers and handle a large number of products. They can do everything from warehousing to shipping to servicing goods after sale. This is one of the most common means of distribution for consumer goods.

- *General line wholesalers* sell to a limited set of retailers, such as sporting goods stores, camera shops, and gourmet kitchen stores. The products extend to all types of merchandise of interest to the type of store.

- *Specialty line wholesalers* handle a very large assortment of a narrow product category, such as greeting cards, jewelry, fishing tackle, or lingerie.

- *Rack jobbers* stock shelves, set up displays, and mark prices. They service many different types of stores, including grocery, drug, convenience, and variety. The products include housewares, health products, beauty aids, and most other mass-marketed nonfood merchandise. More than one rack jobber may service a given store. These middlemen concentrate on fast-moving items, and they usually favor brand names.

Getting a commitment from a rack jobber is a giant step toward successful sales.

• *Brokers* and *manufacturers' representatives* are basically agents. They are often called "sales reps" or "reps." They neither take title to goods nor become involved in warehousing and shipping. They are primarily salespeople. Instead of marking the goods up, they make commissions on sales.

Distributors and reps operate within designated geographic "territories." Most insist upon "exclusive" agencies. This means each manufacturer uses only one per territory, which eliminates conflict and avoids confusion.

After exploring the system, you will know how your product will be distributed, what the mark-up will be, and, perhaps, what certain middlemen think of your concept. This is invaluable information whether you go into business for yourself or try to sell the idea to a company. Your knowledge and consideration of these subjects should be reflected in any presentation. Showing that you have done your homework and know the industry will give you credibility.

As with your financial analysis, your investigation into selling and distribution does not have to be one hundred percent thorough at this time. You are evaluating overall viability of the concept. For now, you only want to decide whether you should keep the idea for further development. If the concept passes this screening, your next round of research and analysis will be much more detailed and comprehensive.

Preliminary Promotional Considerations

While it is too early to make a detailed marketing plan, you should give some thought to any special promotional problems that could increase costs. Can you foresee a need for special educational programs or other merchandising maneuvers to overcome consumers' unfamiliarity with the type of product or to change ingrained behavior patterns? Will such efforts be feasible? Can they be avoided by adapting the product?

Maintenance and Service

Will the product need maintenance or service? How often? Will the need for service affect consumers' buying decisions? How? Who will do the maintenance? Are there companies with existing service branches that you might approach? Can a service industry be started to go along with the product? How new is the technology? Will people be discouraged from buying until the bugs are out? How can this be counteracted?

Legal, Safety, and Environmental Factors

Some other factors to evaluate are legality, safety, and environmental impact. If you have any questions on these matters with regard to your specific concept, consult government agencies, attorneys, or the appropriate experts before investing too much energy or money in your project.

Safety and potential product liability are important for every product, both for humanitarian and business reasons. Sometimes the law spells out specific restrictions, but, in any case, you want to make certain that potentially dangerous features, such as sharp points or toxic coatings, are avoided. Safety considerations apply to toys, tools, cosmetics, furniture, machinery, electrical items, and just about every other product.

Consider Friend Chips, the miniature radio computers for helping people find compatible mates. What are the potential liabilities of a manufacturer if a woman is raped or injured by someone she meets using a Friend Chip? Are dating services ever held liable in such situations? Are people who introduce two of their friends liable for the harm one does to the other?

Legality, rather than safety, may be the issue for some products. Can you fill chocolate Christmas trees with brandy? Do the liquor-sale restrictions apply to spirits in candies? It probably varies from state to state. How will this affect a national sales campaign? Will you have to make different proof candies for each state? If your idea is to sell little bottles of river silt from the Midwest, called "Mississippi Mud," do you have to worry about agricultural states' laws against importation of soils?

What about labeling requirements? What must you tell consumers? Are any warnings or disclaimers necessary?

Finally, do you need to worry about environmental laws and concerns? Will your manufacturing process produce toxic wastes? Certain high-tech industries, such as silicon chips, have been found to endanger water supplies. On a less significant level, say you have an idea for "Can-fetti," pop-top cans that spray confetti ten feet in every direction. If the product takes off, are you creating a mini-environmental problem? How eager would someone be to buy a gag item that requires a substantial clean-up? Or would these be used mostly at office parties, where janitorial service is provided nightly? Is there any possibility of injury to people when the pressurized contents are released? These are the types of questions you must ask—and answer.

Consider not only whether such problems actually exist, but also whether people might think they do. Companies are already reluctant to buy ideas from outside sources, as you will see in Chapter 9. Complications that seem likely to discourage consumers or create corporate headaches can further reduce their interest. Your task is to anticipate and research these questions and evaluate the viability of your concept in light of them.

Stay Flexible and Keep Revising Your Ideas

Even after a full evaluation, it is not always easy to decide what to do with an idea. There are no guaranteed screening procedures for successful new products. The market will always be somewhat unpredictable. The above process will let you know if there are any insurmountable obstacles. If you still think your idea is a great one, why not go with it?

Evaluation is a never-ending process. In researching the viability of your idea, you will learn a great deal. You will generate novel strategies for meeting consumer resistance and think of many different ways to alter and improve your original concept. You will even get notions for other enterprises.

Take the SUPERCOLA idea. Because there is no heavy-duty cola on the market, you think it is a brilliant concept. You begin evaluating. Preliminary taste tests indicate the sugar and caffeine should be increased by ten percent. But your market tests indicate that, in the face of current health concerns, people might object to such increases. They could perceive your wonderful idea for an old-fashioned, syrupy soft drink as unhealthy!

How much caffeine and sugar is in cola, anyway? A little library research reveals the following: Regular colas contain about three to five milligrams per ounce of caffeine. Coffee contains twenty to thirty milligrams per ounce. Therefore, coffee has eight to ten times more caffeine than cola. You can even quadruple the quantity of caffeine in cola and still have less than half the amount found in coffee. So why all the uproar about taking the caffeine out of *colas?*

What about sugar? You find out that a can of regular cola contains approximately 150 calories. If you add ten percent, it will be 165. A Bartlett pear contains 100 calories. A large banana has 115, and a large apple has 125. A Hershey Bar has 220 calories, as does an Almond Joy. A pack of M & M's contains 240, and a Snickers or Milky Way will give you 270 calories each. The extra sugar in SUPERCOLA may not be nutritional, but it is no worse than candy bars. And recent research reveals that sugar is not such a culprit as previously believed. Sugar substitutes may be far more detrimental.

So it seems that cola is not so bad after all. But how will you tell consumers? All the "no caffeine" and "diet" marketing has left the impression that regular colas contain deadly amounts of caffeine and sugar. Will this destroy SUPERCOLA's chances for success before you start? Perhaps you need to reconsider your target. Instead of touting SUPERCOLA as an old-fashioned drink, maybe it should be a "macho" drink. A drink for people who *want* more sugar and caffeine. Maybe you could tie it in with motorcycles or cowboys or football players.

Or perhaps you could keep the original concept, but educate people about the ingredients. Many food products do so. Some tell long, involved stories about their origins. Why not use SUPERCOLA as an educational tool by printing snack food facts right on the cans? You could call this pop journalism "Cold Facts."

In fact, maybe your SUPERCOLA idea is not just a soft drink, but much more. Go back to your brainstorming notes. Perhaps you will find some scrawls and scribbles to help refine or expand the idea. Maybe it is actually a broader concept for using cola containers as a consumers' communication system. It might be a global system, as cola is perhaps the only truly international food. Suppose it becomes "The People's Cola" with messages printed in many different languages.

What would these alternatives cost? Are they feasible? Could "The People's Cola" organize and promote the Global Blackout idea you had for a voluntary lights out around the world? Always consider all possibilities and choose the ones that are best.

Invention Marketing Services

As you can now see, evaluation of new product ideas is hard work. There are companies which claim to be able to do all or part of the process for you. They offer to evaluate, research, patent, and promote ideas and inventions. These firms advertise in many newspapers' and magazines' classifieds. If the number of ads is a reliable indicator, these invention marketing companies are coming into existence at an accelerating pace. One source estimates that 100,000 people consult them annually.

The United States Small Business Administration advises caution in dealing with invention marketing firms. That is good advice. Investigations by the Federal Trade Commission revealed that one firm, which charged fees ranging from $1,000 to $2,000, had only ten clients out of *thirty-five thousand* who made money on their inventions. Another company with thirty thousand clients had only *three* with successful products. The odds of succeeding on your own can't be much worse than that.

At least one state, California, now has laws regulating these invention promoters. Other states may follow. The California legislature expressly stated the reasons why it has passed a strict statute to curb existing practices. It is well worth quoting:

> The Legislature finds that . . . invention developers' services are generally offered for sums ranging from $500 to $5,000 plus either a percentage of the income that may be derived from the sale or marketing of the idea or invention or a partial ownership interest in the idea or invention; . . . that an extremely small number of inventors to whom these invention developers offer their services ever have their products sold or marketed; that there exists in connection with invention development services, sales practices and business methods which have worked a fraud, deceit, imposition, and financial hardship upon many people of this state . . . .

That says it all. In order to combat these practices, the California law regulates solicitation, requires disclosures, and mandates certain contract terms and cancellation procedures.

While there may be some bona fide, competent firms, you may never be sure you have found one. Besides, it is doubtful they can provide anything you could not do cheaper and better for yourself or by hiring outside help on an as-needed basis. This is especially true for presentations. Who is going to be more enthusiastic and better able to describe and demonstrate your concept than you? Further, many of the invention marketing firms have such poor reputations that companies do not give their submissions serious consideration.

If you decide to use an invention promotion company, exercise caution and select it carefully. Send away for the sales literature of a number of firms and carefully compare them.

If any of these services appeals to you, write or call for further, specific information. Insist upon verifiable statistics on the total number of clients the firm has had and, out of these, the number who have actually made money. Ask for names and addresses of these customers and other references and contact them for feedback. Do not settle for a few flashy success stories. Require that the firm supply you with samples of its prior research, successful products, promotional materials, and lists of companies to which products have been submitted. Spot-check the authenticity of any information supplied.

If the invention marketing firm answers your requests with "market breakdowns," "cost analyses," or other general information couched in jargon, look for another firm. Insist upon a full explanation of their methods. Ask for more than one sample of prior product submissions and compare them. Do they contain the same language, with only the names and descriptions of the products plugged in by word processor? If so, each new product is probably not being given individualized attention. Check with a local Better Business Bureau, Chamber of Commerce, or patent attorney for official information and off-the-record scuttlebutt about the firm.

If you decide to contract for the services of an invention marketer, be sure to read the small print. Pin down *precisely* what your payments cover. Will there be extra fees down the line for patent research or writing product descriptions? How many companies will be contacted? Over what period of time? By what means? Make certain that all important items are in writing. Never accept oral assurances about anything. If the firm refuses to put verbal guarantees into a written contract, do not deal with it.

The usual ploy is to encourage you with praise for your idea and promises of riches if you simply send "$278.53 for an initial research report." Next they will need "$976.89 for market analysis and computer evaluation." Then comes some "secondary research and a target company search for only $1580.67," and so on. These firms know that many people will continue to throw good money after bad, especially if they get an abundance of positive feedback, albeit vague and generalized.

In sum, dealing with invention marketing firms is likely to be frustrating, at a minimum. In general, you cannot expect to receive professional service, accurate information, or timely correspondence.

Government Resources

Many federal and state agencies offer services ranging from general guidance to detailed evaluations and direct grants for individual products. The programs change from time to time. A few of the most interesting current government resources are described below.

The Office of Energy-Related Inventions, a division of the National Bureau of Standards, Department of Commerce, will provide free evaluation of non-nuclear energy-related ideas. The program is designed to encourage conservation and alternative sources of energy. The Office may provide research, development, testing, or marketing support. The average grant award is $70,000, and the entire process can take many months. The Office also sponsors National Innovation Workshops, two-day seminars for individual inventors and small businesses on sources of assistance and methods for developing new products. For information write to this agency at the Department of Commerce, Gaithersburg, MD 20899.

The National Science Foundation ("NSF") makes some grants to small businesses with strong capabilities in scientific research and innovative technology. Write NSF at 1800 G St. N.W., Washington, D. C. 20550. Ask for the *Small Business Guide to Federal R&D Funding Opportunities* and information on other programs. The Small Business Innovation Research Program may be especially relevant.

The National Appropriate Technology Assistance Service ("NATAS") provides information and technical assistance in the areas of alternative energy development and commercialization of energy-related new products. NATAS will answer specific technical questions, refer you to private sector sources of assistance, or provide direct business assistance, such as financing, patenting, licensing, and marketing. Write to NATAS at the Department of Energy, Post Office Box 2525, Butte, MT 59702.

The National Technical Information Service was mentioned above. It is a mine of information on numerous subjects, and its services are many and varied. See the Resource Guide for a partial list of its publications. Write for further information.

NTIS's Center for the Utilization of Federal Technology ("CUFT") may be of particular use in evaluating some ideas. CUFT's *Directory of Federal Technology Resources* is a comprehensive guide to over eight hundred laboratories, facilities, technical information centers, and services available to work directly with you in thirty technical areas. The participating agencies will share expertise, equipment, and facilities as a means of maximizing use of federal technology.

See the Resource Guide for a list of the Small Business Administration's Small Business Development Centers, which offer various forms of assistance to those with product or business ideas.

Most states have programs designed to encourage new product endeavors. Write the office of economic development in the state capital for information.

Universities

From time to time universities establish "innovation centers" or programs within their business schools for evaluating new product ideas. Both faculty and students may participate. The centers are often associated with SBA's Small Business Development Centers. Because they are usually government funded, these programs tend to come and go. A current list of some of these centers appears in the Resource Guide. Contact colleges and universities near you to see if they have similar programs. If not, perhaps a professor of a marketing or new products course would be willing to assign evaluation of your product as a class project. Or maybe a student would like to base a research project on it.

Appreciate Failure and Learn from Mistakes

The reasons for new product failure seem to fall into two basic categories. The first revolves around false assumptions, failures to interpret information objectively, or lack of accurate information about the following:

- Consumers' perceptions of their needs and wants

- Appropriate media for promotion

- Ability of market research to predict actual consumer behavior

- Strengths and weaknesses of competing products

- Capability of competitors to imitate success and learn from the errors of others

The second category of reasons for new product failures involves lack of flexibility. It includes:

- Failure to make adjustments in promotion or in the product itself

- Incompetent planning

- Inability to rethink long-range goals in the face of new developments

It is easy to list factors in the abstract, but the eighty to ninety percent failure rate for new product introductions proves that it is not always easy to apply them in practice. Even the largest companies, with huge budgets for obtaining data and analyzing information, often fail spectacularly. Money alone does not ensure success with a new product.

In sum, after all of your research and objective evaluation, you will be back with your hunches and intuition. At least you may now make educated guesses.

The odds are against you. About two thousand new products are introduced each year in supermarkets and drug stores alone. A large percentage do not make it, even after hundreds of millions of dollars have been spent on roll-outs and in marketing and advertising campaigns. They fail for innumerable reasons, including size, shape, name, color, quality, timing, and price. There is even a private Museum of New Products in Naples, New York, owned by a new product consulting firm. It features some memorable failures which prove again that "newness" alone does not guarantee success.

All this is not meant to discourage you, but to convince you not to be afraid to fail. The big companies do it all the time, and they move on to the next project. *Fear of failure only guarantees that you will fail, because it keeps you from taking the first step.*

Appreciate failures. Learn from them. They are inevitable.

Failure is part of the new product game. Do not take it personally or let your ego get involved. Just keep trying. You only need one or two successes to set you up for life. In any event, that is not what really matters to the true idea addict. A need for security is not conducive to the frame of mind usually required for getting great ideas. The ability to tolerate uncertainty is. Most mental mainliners thrive on risk and serendipity. The process, not the result, is top priority. It's the game that counts.

New product development is an uncharted world of adventure. Your failures will provide valuable learning experiences, the foundations of wisdom. Every step you take while getting, refining, developing, and trying to sell an idea is a unique event, an exploration into the unknown. It is not easy or secure. But, as a constant statement of freedom of action and choice, new product creation and development is almost always intense and exciting.

So, now that you have screened and evaluated your ideas and chosen the best one, it is time to act on it. The infinite world of commercial possibility beckons. Do not delay, lest the forces of sychronicity produce someone else who will act first.

CHAPTER 7: THE BIG DECISION: SELL YOUR IDEA OR DO IT YOURSELF

The *Goochy Goo* Chronicles

I need a fantastic label. A petrolatum package that will jump right off the shelf. Make Vaseline look like an old-fashioned medicine. What are the "in" colors? Purple, violet, magnolia, orchid. I'll get super-creative designers. Give them a percentage. Motivation. That's the name of the game . . . . . And better protect the name. Have my cousin, Rick, trademark it. I know one of the lawyers in his firm does that stuff . . . . . What about promo? I'll pass out free samples in the financial district. The media will pick it up, and I'll get tons of publicity. That's free advertising . . . . . What else? Storage. I'll clean out the garage. About time I did that anyway. Probably find the pipe goop and a bunch of old Vaseline jars buried under the mess. I'll just leave 'em there. Ha! I'll literally bury Vaseline under Goochy Goo . . . . . I'll rent a few vans to make deliveries until Goochy Goo gets going and the big rack-jobbers start begging me for the privilege of distributing my all-purpose designer goo. Then one of the big drug or household products companies will buy me out. Hmmmm, I wonder if they'd just buy the idea? Save me from having to go through all the expense and effort of starting my own business. But maybe it's better to get it going on my own. They'll pay much more when the name's established and it has a good track record . . . . . Besides, I want to do it. I've always wanted to be my own boss. Come to think of it,

I've always been the world's greatest admirer of Vas—Whoops!—petroleum jelly . . . . . ♩♩♩ Thank heaven for diaper rash . . . . . ♩♩♫♩

You have figured out *what*. Now you need to know *how*. Your idea has passed through all the review screens. You have evaluated it as worthy of development. The more you research it, the more you like it. You are convinced you have a winner. What's next?

The Big Decision. Once you have a viable idea, you must decide whether to sell the concept or manufacture and distribute the product yourself. You must consider not only your own skills and resources, but also the nature of the product and its suitability for production by an existing company. Is your concept good enough to stand alone and justify the launching of a new business? Or would it best be sold as an extension of the product line of a going concern?

This is the crossroads. You must recheck and refine everything, especially technological and financial feasibility. You must also do some important research on yourself, especially into your interests, entrepreneurial abilities, and financial capabilities.

Know Thyself

What is important to you? What do you like to do? What are you doing now? Ideally, you are proud and happy about your day-to-day existence. You are doing what you believe in, and you are enjoying it. If your present life falls short of this ideal, idea creation and development can be a great way to remedy the situation.

In making the Big Decision, it is wise to examine your objectives and motivations. What do you want to do with your life, and why? Do you believe in your concept, or do you just want to make money? Or both? Do you want to be famous? Be honest. Know thyself. How will development of your concept best serve your goals and beliefs? The more honest you are at this critical time, the more likely you are to make the best decision.

If you don't know what you excel at, it's time to learn. If you don't know what you want to do, it's time to find out. If you aren't doing what you enjoy, it's time to begin.

Creating and playing with ideas is fascinating and fun. Making and marketing a product yourself requires starting a business. Running a company day-to-day, selling, trying to collect money, and having to pay new bills each month can be tedious work, especially if you would rather be inventing, brainstorming, or exploring the mall.

Although starting your own firm can be creative and rewarding, it definitely demands skills and commitments different from those for getting ideas. You must assess whether you have those skills and whether you are willing to make those commitments. Are you really an entrepreneur? Or a manager? What about technical knowledge and competence, not to mention organizational and leadership skills? Even if you have these talents, you must decide if you want to be using them in starting and running a demanding and potentially risky new enterprise. Maybe you need the security of your present job and want to create new products as a pleasurable and potentially rewarding hobby. Perhaps you should consider a partner. In any case, do not try to take shortcuts through this agonizing area of self-evaluation. Know thyself.

To Sell or Not to Sell

Either way, developing an idea is a big commitment. But, since selling the idea involves less investment of time, energy, and money, your efforts might logically begin here. There are several distinct advantages to pursuing this route. Although you will receive only a small percentage of the profits, you will do so with almost no financial risk. Your contribution consists almost entirely of your idea and the time and money you spend on your prototype and presentation.

You will not have to perfect, protect, package, promote, distribute, or sell the product yourself. Experienced professionals will perform all of these functions, and at no direct cost to you. The firm's advertising and marketing will benefit your product.

If you sell to an established company, the chances of others being able to steal the idea are greatly reduced. This is because "your" company will probably be big enough to capture a large portion of the market before anyone else can start to think about copying the concept. Being first on the market is usually an advantage. It places your product's name foremost in consumers' minds and intimidates potential knock-off artists. Also, a large company will have the legal and financial muscle to protect against any patent and trademark infringements.

But selling your idea to an existing company is not necessarily the best way to proceed. There are disadvantages. Your product may be unsuitable for sale to a company. You may find that no firms are interested. Or perhaps you would simply rather start a business around your concept and stay in charge of its development and promotion.

Selling the idea sounds easy. It isn't. If the product is not successful, you may receive nothing. Even if you succeed, you will receive only a small percentage of the revenues generated from sales. Also, since established companies often move very slowly, you may have to wait a long time before you receive any money. It is possible to negotiate for advances against future royalties, but this is not common.

Moreover, there is no guarantee that the company will develop the product as you envisioned. When you sell a concept, you no longer call the shots. If you have strong feelings about how it should look or what it should be called or how it ought to be promoted, such loss of control is something to consider *before* you make your decision.

Some of these disadvantages can be reduced or eliminated by contract. For example, you may negotiate a position as a consultant during development of the product, or a right to develop it yourself or sell it to someone else if the company has not begun marketing it within a certain time. You probably won't have much bargaining power, so if any of the above disadvantages is absolutely unacceptable, you had better think twice before putting any of your brainchildren up for adoption.

Sometimes the inherent nature of a concept, its size, or its suitability for a specific industry is such that you have no real choice. If you have come up with a functioning design for a new automobile transmission system, you will head directly for Detroit. Directly after seeing your patent attorney, that is.

But even if you were not intimidated by the scope of the transmission project, what about money? Who is going to finance it? You would have to raise millions of dollars of venture capital just to get started, and by then your competitors (GM, Ford, Chrysler, Toyota, Mercedes, etc.) would be working on ways to get around your patent. Or maybe they would just copy your concept and count on their legal and financial clout to overpower you in the patent courtroom.

The Heart of the Business Plan

Preparing a good preliminary business plan is an invaluable aid in making the "sell vs. do" decision. And, after you decide, the plan is an essential tool for starting a company or using as input for selling the concept.

There are dozens of books on how to start a business. Most discuss preparation of a business plan. This book will highlight the parts of a plan that are particularly relevant to the Big Decision. A typical business plan looks like this:

- Section 1 -   Summary
- Section 2 -   The Company
- ♥ Section 3 -   The Product
- ♥ Section 4 -   The Market
- ♥ Section 5 -   Distribution
- ♥ Section 6 -   Projections
- Section 7 -   Management and Personnel
- Section 8 -   Investment Analysis

Sections 3 through 6 are the heart of the business plan. For making the "sell vs. do" decision, they comprise the topics to research and know as well as possible. The following case study illustrates how you might do this for a small-scale new product idea.

 ## Letter To The President

Say you are a conservationist. You have been trying to come up with a concept for a convenience item which enhances, rather than litters, the environment. People today never seem to have enough time. As a result, we have TV dinners, disposable diapers, One-Minute Managers, instant this, instant that, instant everything. You have searched the kitchen, the office, the farm, the forest, everywhere, and have not found an idea that satisfies you. You are ready to give up your infant career as inventor and devote all of your spare time to the environmental movement. In fact, you have been meaning to write a letter to the President for some time, urging him to support tougher standards for toxic wastes. But you have been too busy.

Early the next morning you wake up with a flash. You have a great idea for a new product. It is already elaborately detailed. It goes something like this, and it illustrates that we often get our best ideas in areas we know and care about:

One thing just about everyone wants to do is write a letter to the President. But, if you have never done it before, it is actually a rather complicated and time-consuming task. You have to find the right address, write the letter, mail it, and wonder if it does any good. So, even though this is a free country and you will not be sent to the salt mines for communicating with your leader, very few of us ever do it. And even if you *have* done it before, it is still such an ordeal. So inconvenient!

That's it! The concept strikes you like a lightning bolt. It's a true time-saver. A ready-to-send "Letter to the President." It will be an attractively packaged convenience item people can purchase at the drug store, the supermarket, the 7-Eleven, or anywhere. The slogan will be, "Just sign and send." It will come in a clear plastic bag, with the letter visible on one side, and the envelope, addressed to the President, visible on the other. There will be a stamp on the envelope, so it is truly ready to send. The consumer can even sign and seal it while waiting in the checkout line. Now that's efficient use of time.

You jump out of bed and rush to your desk. You grab pen and paper and make a preliminary sketch. It looks so good, you type up the letter and envelope. You are getting excited. You get a plastic sandwich bag from the kitchen. Next you make a label to staple the bag closed and punch a hole so it can hang on a J-hook in the store. There it is! A product. Or, at least, a prototype. It took less than an hour to make.

It appears so simple. You think you could have it on the market in a week. You can't wait to show your friends. Go ahead. Get excited. You have come up with a great idea, and you deserve to feel happy and proud. Not only that, you are an hour late for work.

Over the next few days you share your idea with trusted friends and other environmentalists. They tell you how great it is and help you come up with refinements. You are getting more and more excited and eager to go ahead. But what do you do next? A business plan—the product, the market, distribution, projections.

You will be working on all of these simultaneously. Start with the product. What really is your product? Is it a letter? A gimmick? A political statement? Are you selling convenience or cuteness? Is your idea for just one letter or for a whole line of them, covering topics such as defense, the deficit, abortion, gun control, or school prayer? Should you give it a catchy name, like "The Instant Citizen"? After much soul-searching and brainstorming with friends, you decide the product is "The Letter to the President," just as you originally conceived it.

You considered doing two letters, one "for" and one "against." They would hang side by side and offer a choice. But this could expose you to negative criticism as an exploiter of an important issue. Let someone else come out with the "other" letter. It will become a race, an event. It will focus attention on an important issue. The media will keep score, and your business will get lots of free publicity.

Having made this decision, you start making a final

prototype and researching financial feasibility. You will need accurate estimates for the following:

- Production costs:
  - Materials
  - Manufacturing

- Operating costs:
  - Promotion
  - Freight
  - Overhead
  - Profit
  - Distribution costs

You begin by finding out how much the materials will cost. Get the Yellow Pages. Call a few printers. Request prices for printing various quantities of the letter, envelope, and label. Ask what the quantity breaks are. Price large quantities, such as 1,000, 5,000, and 10,000. This will ensure a prompt response. If you ask for a price on 100, they may not call back.

Next, get prices for plastic bags. You learn they are distributed by paper suppliers. Request quotes for the same quantities. Also get prices for boxes that will hold twelve of the packaged letters and shipping cartons that will hold ten boxes.

Now figure materials costs for 1,000, 5,000, or 10,000.

LETTER TO THE PRESIDENT
PRODUCTION COSTS: MATERIALS

Materials (per letter)	1,000	5,000	10,000
Letter	$.02	$.015	$.01
Envelope	.04	.035	.03
Label	.035	.03	.02
Plastic Bag	.015	.01	.005
Boxes	.02	.015	.01
Shipping Cartons	.02	.015	.005
First Class Stamp	.22	.22	.22
Total Materials Costs:	$.37	$.34	$.30

Next, work on manufacturing costs: You need to find out how long it takes to make one letter, so you try to duplicate the manufacturing process on a small scale. You set up the materials and time yourself while assembling packages and boxing them for shipment. You were trying to go at a normal working speed, but you think you might be faster than most people, and you certainly are more motivated. Therefore, you have a few friends and relatives try their hands at it, and you take the average time for everyone, adding a few seconds to cover routine delays. Using a fair wage, you estimate labor for packing and boxing will remain constant at about 5 cents per letter. Adding this to the materials costs, you have the total costs of production:

LETTER TO THE PRESIDENT
PRODUCTION COSTS

	1,000	5,000	10,000
Materials	$.37	$.34	$.30
Manufacturing	.05	.05	.05
Total Production Costs	$.42	$.39	$.35

Onward to operating costs. By talking with some advertising people, you learn that the sky's the limit for promotion. So you decide to let the uniqueness of the product generate its own publicity. Maybe you will send out a few press releases and see if the media will provide free coverage. Just to play it safe, you decide to allocate a minimum of 1 cent per letter for promotion.

You call a few parcel services and truck companies and quickly determine that it will average about 2 cents per letter for shipping.

Finally, you must figure your overhead. Because you will be operating out of your house and garage, these costs will be nominal, at least at the outset. In fact, you may be able to deduct some of your utilities and other house expenses. In any case, we are not talking great sums here. Say you produce and sell 5,000 letters. At 5 cents per letter, the total is only $250. That sounds too low. The phone and utilities alone will be at least that. So you decide that 10 cents each for 1,000 and 5,000 and 9 cents each for 10,000 are more realistic estimates, at least until your business gets so big that you have to move it to fancier quarters.

That makes the total operating costs for promotion, shipping, and overhead come to 13 cents per letter:

LETTER TO THE PRESIDENT
OPERATING COSTS

	1,000	5,000	10,000
Promotion	$.01	$.01	$.01
Freight	.02	.02	.02
Overhead	.10	.10	.09
Total Operating Costs	$.13	$.13	$.12

Adding production and operating expenses for the various quantities, the total projected costs per letter are:

LETTER TO THE PRESIDENT
TOTAL COSTS

	1,000	5,000	10,000
Production Costs	$.42	$.39	$.35
Operating Costs	.13	.13	.12
Total Costs	$.55	$.52	$.47

By starting with 10,000, economies of scale and quantity breaks will save you 8 cents per letter. You decide to go for it. Now add your profit. How much do you want to make? You find out that the standard practice of small greeting card companies for items such as this is to add on from 30 to 50 percent over costs of production. You decide to keep it low and use 35 percent, which will give you some 17 cents per letter. That sounds reasonable. Adding that to the 47-cent production costs gives you a grand total of 64 cents for each letter. This is your selling price to the distributors:

The Big Decision

LETTER TO THE PRESIDENT
PRICE TO DISTRIBUTORS

Manufacturer's Costs	$.47
Manufacturer's Profit	.17
Total Price to Distributors	$.64

Meanwhile, you have been researching how greeting cards are sold and distributed. You have learned that wholesale mark-ups vary between 20 and 30 percent. You decide to use the average, or 25 percent. Multiply 64 cents times 0.25 and you get 16 cents. Add this on, and the total now comes to 80 cents. This is the price to the retailer:

LETTER TO THE PRESIDENT
PRICE TO RETAILERS

Price to Distributors	$.64
Distributors' Mark-Up	.16
Total Price to Retailers	$.80

You noticed that some middlemen spoke of "mark-ups," and others talked of "margins." They are both ways of referring to the difference between price paid and price received. But what's the difference? You get confused and stop for a moment to think about it. If a middleman buys an item for $1 and sells it for $1.25, that's a 25 percent mark-up, because he adds 25 percent to his cost. Divide 25 cents by $1, and the result is 25 percent. He starts with his cost and marks it up 25 cents.

The "margin" is computed from the opposite direction. You start the calculation with the selling price and then subtract cost. In the above example, the result would be 25 cents. Then you figure what percent that number is of the selling price. Divide 25 cents by $1.25, and you get 20 percent. Voila! The margin. In brief: Mark-up is the difference expressed as a percentage of price paid, and margin is the difference expressed as a percentage of price received. It is really not very complicated at all.

Now that you have that straightened out, you continue.

The distributors informed you that retailers will mark up between 50 and 100 percent, depending on the type of store. So call it 75 percent on the average. Multiply 80 cents times 0.75, and the result is 60 cents. Adding this on to, or marking up, the 80-cent price paid by retailers, the total now comes to $1.40 per letter. That's the ballpark price to the consumer:

LETTER TO THE PRESIDENT
PRICE TO THE CONSUMER

Manufacturer's Costs	$.47
Manufacturer's Profit	.17
Distributors' Mark-Up	.16
Retailers' Mark-Up	.60
Total Price to Consumers	$1.40

A dollar forty. Good grief! Your first reaction is that this is much too high. People ought to be able to express their sentiments for less than that. You are afraid that no one will buy the letter at that price. How can you lower it? Eliminate the stamp. That chops 22 cents from materials and 1 cent from labor, which will work out to around a 68-cent reduction in the retail price. A general rule of thumb well worth remembering is that a one-dollar change in production costs will change the selling price of an item by about three dollars, depending on the specific product and standard mark-ups for the industry.

LETTER TO THE PRESIDENT
REVISED PRICE TO THE CONSUMER

Materials (minus 22¢ for stamp)	$.08
Manufacturing (minus 1¢)	.04
Operating Costs	.12
Manufacturer's Cost	.24
Manufacturer's Profit (35 percent)	.09
Price to Distributors	.33
Distributors' Mark-Up (25 percent)	.08
Price to Retailers	.41
Retailers' Mark-Up (75 percent)	.31
Total Price to Consumers	$.72

This means the Letter to the President can now be retailed for about 69 to 79 cents, depending on individual retailers' mark-ups. That makes it feasible, you think.

But is it still a convenience item? Will people buy it? Sure. People are used to putting on their own postage.

Next consideration: What is the market? The distributors think it will be a hot item for a year at most. Some thought you could expect to sell half a million to a million. They want to handle it, so distribution is no problem.

The final business plan item is projections. This usually means long-range estimates for things like sales, changes in costs, capital requirements, debt, and so on. None of these is relevant to the letter, as you believe it will be a short-lived fad.

You should now have the necessary information for making the Big Decision. Do you sell the concept to an existing company or start your own business? Ask yourself questions such as:

- Why do I want to do this?

- Will I enjoy dealing with suppliers, ordering paper, looking after printing jobs, and so on?

- Will I like supervising laborers folding paper and stuffing and stapling plastic bags?

- Will I like dealing with distributors and wondering when or if they will pay?

- Will I enjoy the publicity if this gets into the news?

- Do I believe in this project?

- Will I feel good about making and selling "The Letter to the President"?

You ponder these questions for a long time and finally decide to do it yourself. It is definitely an easy starter. It could be fun, and you think it is socially redeeming. It might even make a profit.

Next is a scenario for a much more substantial project. You recently bought a computer. You love it. But you don't like having to take one hand off the keyboard to use the "mouse." You get frustrated. Then angry. You want to return it. Suddenly, as your frustration and frenzy peak, you get a flash of inspiration. Why not put the mouse on the floor? You can operate it with your feet and keep your hands free to type. What a great idea!

You start to get excited about this concept. You begin designing a total approach to foot-controlled computer operations. Wait a minute. Not so fast. You had better first do a little research and evaluation. You discover there is nothing like it on the market yet. It passes all the other preliminary tests and screens. You think it just might be a fantastic money-maker. But, in what form?

Are you going to start a computer hardware company and get into manufacturing and all that goes with it? Or should you just develop the concept for sale to an existing firm? Once again, it's the Big Decision, which means it's time to work up a preliminary business plan. As always, the middle sections are the ones to concentrate on: the product, the market, distribution, projections.

What exactly is the product? Is it a keyboard on the floor or a foot pedal similar to those for sewing machines, pianos, and shop tools? Is it an accelerator like people are used to using in cars? You make a preliminary decision to design it as a four-way switch for cursor control and scrolling. Instead of having a handle like video game controls, yours will be a little box for the foot to move around. Whichever direction the foot moves, so will the cursor move. Hit the top to scroll, and step on it to control velocity. "Step On It," that's a good name.

So you sketch it out and start playing around with names. Footmouse? The Cat? Foot Cursor? Ground Cursor? Ground Control? Hey! "Ground Control," that's it! You check these names in the *Trademark Register* at the library. Very interesting. "Footmouse" belongs to a California company. "Cat" is registered by Xerox. Xerox! Wow! "Ground Control" is not taken. Whew!

You start to make a simple mock-up, but quickly realize that something this technical and complicated requires a full-blown working prototype. So you ask around at computer stores and locate a handyman/engineer/designer to build it. You collaborate closely with him and discover that it is not so easy to design something for the foot. You study ergonomics, the science of how the body moves, and conclude that Ground Control should also be a foot rest. It should be positioned at an angle, like the accelerator of an automobile.

You discuss the idea with close friends. One of them is a country music fan and tells you to check out the pedal steel instrument. It has numerous foot pedals and knee bars which produce the whines and wails of country music. So you research this and start thinking of elaborate whole-body systems, until another friend brings you back down to earth. Such a space-age product is great if the Pentagon is paying for it, but the start-up costs put it way beyond your abilities and aspirations, at least initially.

During your prototype development, several people tell you Ground Control is a great idea for a video game. This sidetracks you for a few weeks, talking to game designers and manufacturers. But, again one of your friends grounds you, and you get back to the original notion. It is time to refine the product with your engineer and get it working.

Meanwhile, you have been busy with the Yellow Pages and have visited various suppliers and fabricators. You have assembled the following cost estimates for manufacturing Ground Control:

The Big Decision

GROUND CONTROL
COSTS OF PRODUCTION

	5,000	10,000	50,000
Materials	$20.00	$18.00	$12.00
Manufacturing	35.00	30.00	15.00
Promotion	25.00	10.00	5.00
Freight	5.00	3.00	1.00
Miscellaneous Costs	20.00	15.00	7.00
Overhead	35.00	30.00	15.00
Total	$140.00	$106.00	$55.00

It is obvious that for a product this complex, you have to make a certain minimum quantity to produce them at a reasonable cost. Now plug in your profit of, say, 25 percent, and the prices to distributors come to approximately $175, $133, and $69, depending on the quantity manufactured. Add on the distributor's mark-up, another 25 percent, and the prices to retailers come to about $219, $166, and $86.

Finally, give the retailers their mark-up. Because the computer industry is so new, this can vary from about 15 to 50 percent, depending on the type of product and the class of store. So you plug in 30 percent, and the selling prices for the various quantities come to around $285, $216, and $112.

You are sure people will pay $112 for Ground Control, but you have some doubts about the $285. That will require some market research.

What is the market for Ground Control, anyway? Will everyone want one? Is it something for home, or office, or both? How many will sell at different price levels? And how in the world are you going to answer all of these questions?

Well, you can guess. Or you can hire a market research company, which means you buy someone else's educated guesses. You meet with a few firms and get estimates ranging from $5,000 to $25,000 for "preliminary testing and analysis." You decide you would prefer to make your own guesses.

Back to the library! You want to know how many people own computers and how many computers are predicted to sell for the next five years. You plunge into this research and find an abundance of data. After wading through it, you finally surface with the necessary information for projecting computers in use, plus sales and replacements for the next five years. The total is approximately ten million. This means there will be an annual average of two million computer owners who will be potential purchasers of Ground Control units.

Now you need to estimate how many of these will actually buy your device. You will do a little basic market research and plug your numbers into the "Basic Projection Table," which looks like this:

BASIC PROJECTION TABLE

PROJECTED PRICE

	Low	Medium	High
	$___	$___	$___

PROJECTED SALES

Low

Medium

High

This simple market research tool can be used for almost anything. It is surprisingly accurate when the product is price elastic and the forces of supply and demand are operating efficiently. To arrive at the figures, show your working prototype to at least 100 people. Let them use it on their computers. Have them fill out a short questionnaire. Ask questions like the following: Would they buy one? At what price would they not buy? How would they improve it? Do they like the name? And so on. You can gather a surprising amount of data in this way.

From your sample data, compute percentages for how many people will buy at the various selling prices. Apply these percentages to the information you have put together on computer owners and insert the results into the basic projection table. The results of your computer market and consumer research are as follows:

GROUND CONTROL
PROJECTED ANNUAL SALES

PRICE

SALES:	Low $112	Medium $216	High $285
Low	10,000	7,500	5,000
Medium	30,000	20,000	10,000
High	500,000	400,000	300,000

Voila! The market. Or, at least, the projected potential market for Ground Control. This is a very preliminary analysis for the present purpose, and it can be refined later. Taking the medium projections for sales and price, you figure that you could sell about twenty thousand units per year over the first five years at $216 each. That works out to total gross sales of $4.3 million annually. Not bad. Be more conservative and predict a medium/low or even a low/low outcome. That's still not bad.

It also means someone will have to produce and distribute trucks full of Ground Controls to stores all over the country. So you take your model and your figures and talk to some distributors. They are enthusiastic and give you informal commitments to take on your product.

That covers three of the four critical business plan sections. The fourth, projections, requires expertise in accounting and tax matters. It involves capital requirements, start-up costs, break-even points, gross revenues, net profits or losses, inventory considerations, interest and debt service calculations, and large amounts of other technical information. You have it all described in the many books on how to start a business. You decide that it is much too complicated for you, and you would just as soon sell the Ground Control concept to an existing computer hardware manufacturer and receive some equitable royalty.

That's it. You have made the Big Decision. Once again, it is during the research and preparation of the heart of the business plan. So now you will get your presentation ready to show to a few target companies. You have a working model. You have a lot of information on the product and costs of production. You have a reasonable grasp of the market, and you have a range of projections for expected consumer behavior based on realistic price variations. Finally, you have distribution in the bag.

FRIEND CHIPS

This is the final episode in the Big Decision mini-series. You are walking in the woods one day. You are a little lonely and are thinking how nice it would be to know if there are any possible companions nearby. Then all of a sudden, WHAM! The complete idea for "Friend Chips" hits you—a tiny computer chip, linked to a miniature radio transceiver that sends and receives personal information for the purpose of matching people in close proximity with compatible friends, companions, lovers, and so on.

You run a three-minute mile back to your car, speed home, and start calling your friends who are "into" computers. Is it feasible? They don't know. So the next day you see an expert and find out it is. You get several quotes from computer and electronics manufacturers for the costs of start-up and production. You discover that the start-up costs alone are over a million dollars, and that does not even include any allocations for promotion and marketing. So you visit a few venture capitalists who specialize in high-tech fields. You soon learn that the Friend Chips concept is too innovative for even the most venturesome of venture capitalists.

Thus, the Big Decision is made for you, before you even begin any in-depth research. You will have to sell the idea to someone big and already well established in the manufacturing and merchandising of consumer electronics products. Therefore, you continue your research with a focus on putting together a presentation for such a company. Simultaneously, you begin looking for the most futuristic and innovative firms in this field.

You hire an expert to write a technical description of the product. An artist draws some pictures and a logo and makes some mock-ups in the form of watches, beepers, jewelry, and so on.

You begin researching the market by getting some numbers from the computer dating companies and figuring out the amounts spent on personal classifieds in the various papers. You talk to singles groups, teenagers, and senior citizens' associations. It is obvious that there is a potential market for a new method of bringing compatible people together. The exact dimensions of the market are unquantifiable, but it seems like the kind of thing nearly everyone would want.

Distribution is going to be something of a problem because no one will be the first to buy a device that requires there to be a large number in existence for them to work. So part of your marketing and promotion plan will include giving away enough Friend Chips so that a critical mass is achieved and they work so well that nobody will want to be without one. After that, the potential for imaginative merchandising is limitless. Actually, they will sell themselves, mostly by word of mouth. What was perceived as luxury will soon be seen as necessity. Marketing expenses will be zero, and the money saved can be used to perfect and expand the capabilities of the product.

Projections for a product such as this sound more like science fiction than objective business fact. Nevertheless, you put together a professional presentation, compile a target list of potential customers, and immediately begin to act on your decision to sell the Friend Chip concept to an existing firm.

Summary

These three examples yield some interesting insights. The relatively simple Letter to the President required a great deal of preliminary research. It did not take inventions. Just inventiveness.

The more complicated Ground Control required a moderate amount of research on the product and the market, but hardly any on the means of distribution. It will require an invention. It was decided fairly early to try to sell the idea to a large company which could do the manufacturing, create the demand, and plug it into an existing distribution system.

Finally, the futuristic Friend Chips, by far the most complicated of the three, required very little preliminary research. This idea will require inventions for enhancing communication, and it may eventually lead to innovations in human behavior. You knew from the start that it would have to be done by a biggie. So you put most of your efforts into the presentation—into marketing your idea.

There are some significant laws of new product development to be found here: The more complicated the product and expensive the start-up, the more likely you are to decide to sell the idea, rather than try to manufacture and market it yourself. This is not an ironclad law, as many entrepreneurs have developed complicated and complex products and made fortunes. What we do not know is whether they did so after being turned down by big companies that were potential buyers of their ideas.

Many times an entrepreneur will start a company around a new product idea with the sole intention of selling out for big money once the business is established. This may be a way of sidestepping the Big Decision, but it is also starting out in a state of limbo. Companies begun in this way may fail due to lack of commitment and direction.

Therefore, even if selling the business is your ultimate goal, you must still be thoroughly committed to starting and running a successful operation. Celestial Seasonings, the herbal tea company, was begun in 1969 by enterprising hippies in Boulder, Colorado. They had the right idea at the right time, plus extraordinarily effective graphics. The founders sold out ten years later to General Mills for millions.

You might ask what keeps big firms from just stealing successful ideas and entering the market with their own similar products. Unless the product is patented or otherwise protected, the answer is nothing. In practice, it is often easier and more desirable for a larger company to acquire an established name and a going concern, along with the people who got it going.

If your idea is controversial or ahead of its time, starting and selling a business may be the only way it can be sold. Established companies are often unwilling to inaugurate controversial or futuristic ventures, but will purchase them after they have been proven. The sometimes painful irony of this method is that you are pouring yourself into something you will eventually have to leave.

In sum, there are many ways to go about developing a great idea. The more you learn from your product and market research, the more thoroughly you investigate distribution, the more intelligently you project the future for your product, and the more closely you examine your personal resources and motivations, the better you will be able to select and start out on the optimal path.

CHAPTER 8: PROTECT YOUR IDEAS FROM OTHERS AS OTHERS PROTECT THEIR IDEAS FROM YOU

The *Goochy Goo* *Chronicles*

"What did you say, Rick? Somebody objected to my trademark application? Who? . . . . . Gucci! The Italian designer? Yeah, the expensive leather stuff with the little upside-down G's Sanskritted all over it. What do they care about petroleum jelly? . . . . . Oh, they're into cosmetics now. Mass market. Jumbo drug stores. The whole bit . . . . . Sure, sure. The big boys protect their names at all times. I know I'm calling Goochy Goo 'The Designer Jelly.' You think that's what they didn't like? . . . . . They want me to what? Change the name? No way! Let 'em take me to court. I'll get enough free publicity to overtake Vaseline in a year . . . . . What? That's not how it works? I may not be able to get a trademark? That's not fair. I thought the trademark laws were to protect me. Huh? They only really work for companies with lots of money and lawyers? Holy cow, what should I do, Rick? . . . . . Give up? Get my job back? No. Just because they're bigger than me, I'm not going to throw in the towel. At least not without a fight. How much will it cost to fight this? It could go to several million? Who do you think I am, the Pentagon?" . . . . . I know what I'll do. I'm going to sell Goochy Goo to someone a lot bigger than Gucci. Then we'll give 'em a real fight. Heck, why doesn't Gucci just buy

Goochy Goo? He could really do a designer jelly: "Gucci
Goo!" *It will preserve and beautify his handbags better than
most chemical products. It's almost the same thing as mineral
oil, the ultimate leather conditioner* ..... ♪♪ *Thank heaven
..... for nothing. I've got to fly to New York. Fast.*

When people think of protection, they usually want to
know how to safeguard their own rights. But others have
patents, trademarks, copyrights, trade secrets, and other rights
that you must be careful not to infringe. As you learn about
legal protections, remember that they not only help you, but
may also restrain you.

This chapter introduces you to major points about
protecting your ideas. It is not a how-to guide for your own
patenting and other legal work. Do not expect to become an
expert at law. If and when you need legal advice, get a
professional. Lawyers unravel complexities and spot issues
that you simply will not recognize without legal training. Don't
be like the inventor who said he didn't need an attorney
because the company he was dealing with had two. Legal
consultation before a problem arises is often a wise investment.

Attorneys fees do not have to be high, and you can help
control them. Lawyers usually charge by time spent. If you are
organized and concise, less time will be required. Give the
attorney an idea of how much you can afford. You can also
reduce costs by using attorneys who have experience in the
particular area of law. Lawyers specialize. Those with expertise
know the field and spend less time researching for answers.
Shop around. Don't be afraid to ask questions about a lawyer's
background. Bar associations can refer you to private attorneys
who give inexpensive initial consultations.

While you should leave the real legal work to lawyers, it is
useful to have an overall view of the law relevant to new
products. This will enable you to ask the right questions,
recognize potential problem areas, know when to seek advice,
and communicate more effectively with an attorney.

Patents

Is your invention worth patenting? Is it even patentable? Will a patent help you sell the concept? Will you do your own application, or would you rather work on other tasks? How good is patent protection anyway?

There are three types of patents: Utility, design, and plant. Utility patents are what people normally mean when they speak of patents. They cover the mechanical designs and functions of inventions. Design patents cover the ornamental or visual aspects of manufactured articles, rather than their structures or utilitarian features. Plant patents protect new varieties of vegetables, flowers, trees, shrubs, and other plants.

There are over 100,000 patent applications each year, and only about fifty to sixty percent are granted. Although design and plant patents are somewhat simpler than utility patents to obtain, the process is never easy.

The standards for utility patents are especially difficult to meet. In a nutshell, the invention must be new, useful, and not obvious. Newness has to do with whether and when the invention was described in print or made available for sale. Usefulness means the invention actually performs a utilitarian purpose. Nonobviousness means the invention would not be obvious to someone having ordinary skill in the field. For example, the substitution of one material for another and changes in size are normally not patentable. Methods of doing business, printed matter, and certain nuclear inventions cannot be patented. Nor can mere ideas or suggestions.

To patent or not to patent, that is the question. In the vast majority of cases, applying for a patent is a waste of time and money. It can even be an obstacle to accomplishing other necessary tasks for getting a product on the market. Patents have a certain aura or mystique. Most people think that getting a patent is a seal of approval or guarantee of success. Nothing could be further from the truth.

Drawbacks to Patents

Patents represent a deal between you and the government. In exchange for making the details of your invention public, the government gives you the exclusive right to make, use, and sell it for a period of time. Anyone else who wants to do so must get your permission. This system is supposed to encourage progress because inventive people will share their discoveries knowing they will profit from their use. Nice theory. In practice it is quite another story.

First of all, getting a patent is a long, expensive, difficult, bureaucratic procedure. It usually takes about two to three years from start to finish. The fees for applying and paying a patent agent or attorney can amount to several thousand dollars. The attorney or agent must conduct a search, fill out the application forms, frame the description and claims for your patent correctly, obtain a Patent and Trademark Office-style drawing, and negotiate over which of your claims will be allowed.

Yes, you *can* do it yourself, if you really want to spend three years of your life engaged in one of the most complicated and arcane pursuits known to humankind. There are several books on the market that point the way. Getting involved in doing your own patenting is, however, almost certain to dilute your creative energy and distract you from other steps you should be taking to sell your idea.

The part of the patent known as the "claims" is critical. The claims are what the Patent Examiners rely upon to judge patentability, and they are what determine the extent of the patent once it is granted. Framing them too broadly or too narrowly can adversely affect your success in obtaining or enforcing a patent. The requirements are highly technical, and stating the claims is an art that most people, even professional inventors, are not equipped to handle well.

Second, even if you can get one, patents often do not provide very good protection. This is true for a variety of reasons. If someone infringes your patent, the only way to enforce your rights is to bring a lawsuit. You would like to get an injunction to stop sales of the infringing product. However, such injunctions are rarely granted, especially in the first suit to protect the patent. This means that the other party can continue selling the product while you litigate the case, which can take years. If you win, you will get monetary damages, but you are then faced with the problem of collecting them. This can be quite costly and frustrating.

Furthermore, just having a patent is no guarantee that it will hold up in court. Whomever you sue will try to prove that it should never have been granted, and, according to one survey, there is a seventy percent chance that your patent will be held invalid.

To get the patent, you must publicly reveal the details of your invention. While competitors cannot copy it exactly, they will know how it works. They may, in fact, be able to "invent around" it legally by changing a few details. For this reason, patents are not even sought for many otherwise patentable products, especially in fast-moving, highly technical fields where secrecy is deemed more valuable than possible patent protection.

Patents protect only the "claims." If you filed before having fully developed the concept, you may have overlooked important claims that should have been included. Your competitors will be free to use and, perhaps, even patent the new ones.

Many people assume that a patented item will sell itself. This is simply not the case. Only a small percentage of the tens of thousands of patents granted each year are ever marketed as real products.

United States patents have virtually no effect in foreign countries. Almost every nation has its own laws, and you must file separately wherever you want protection. This can be prohibitively expensive.

In short, trying to get a patent can sidetrack you. Trying to enforce one can bankrupt you.

Advantages of Patents

Despite all the drawbacks, there are some good reasons for obtaining a patent:

- It may discourage others from trying to compete with you.

• In attempting to sell your idea to an existing manufacturer, the fact that you have applied for or obtained a patent makes you appear serious, knowledgeable, and confident in the uniqueness of your product.

• The patent itself can be an effective document for demonstrating exactly what the product is.

• A patent provides some assurance that others will not show up and claim ownership of your idea.

The Ordeal of Getting a Patent

If you want to apply for a patent, start the process immediately. The person with the patent, not the first with the idea, is entitled to protection. Begin by consulting the publications listed in Chapter 5 and in the Resource Guide at the end of the book. Decide with the help of a patent attorney or agent whether it is worthwhile to apply for patent protection.

The Patent and Trademark Office will send you free lists of attorneys and registered agents arranged by location. You can also find listings in the Yellow Pages under "Patent Attorneys and Agents." Although there is no directory for specialists in particular fields, you should address this matter before hiring anyone. A reputable attorney or agent will refer you to someone else if your project is outside his or her area of expertise. Patent agents can serve you as well as lawyers, and their services are less expensive. Since they are not attorneys at law, however, they would not be able to represent you in any litigation.

It is a good idea to keep a log of your progress during the period you conceive of and play with your idea. This will help establish your priority should it ever become an issue. A comprehensive description is found in *You and the Patenting Process,* available from the Department of Energy, Assistant General Counsel for Patents, Washington, D. C. 20545. Before applying for a patent, you can file an official "disclosure document" with the Patent and Trademark Office briefly explaining your invention. Although this filing will help establish priority, it provides no patent protection of any kind. For further details, consult *The Disclosure Document Program,* a pamphlet available from the Patent and Trademark Office.

Even if you do not intend to get a patent, you may want to do a search to be certain your product would not infringe others' rights. You can do a preliminary search yourself, and this can be interesting. Looking at other patents will give you additional ideas and broaden your background and exposure to inventions in your field.

The best place to do a complete search is in the Search Room of the Patent and Trademark Office in Arlington, Virginia. There are patent collections in Patent Depository Libraries throughout the United States, but they are not as complete or well classified. These libraries are listed in the Resource Guide. Some of them have online computer data bases to facilitate the process. The library staffs will help you. If you pay an agent or attorney for a search, he or she will arrange for it to be done by a specialist in Arlington. The cost will be about three to five hundred dollars.

There are practical alternatives to getting a patent that may offer just as much protection. If a company can be the first on the market, make the most early sales, and quickly get a leadership image, imitators and potential competitors may be discouraged. Therefore, the time and money saved in not applying for a patent may be better spent in arranging quick manufacture and thorough distribution.

When it comes to protection, everyone thinks of patents. However, depending on the product, copyrights, trademarks, and common law considerations can be far more significant.

Copyright

Suppose you wanted to use the song, "The Great Pretender," in developing and marketing The Great Pet Tender. Do you need permission from the Platters or whoever currently owns the copyright? Can you use a modified version without getting permission? Can you be sued? What are the chances of winning? How much might you have to pay? For a product requiring so much start-up expense, it is best to cover all angles in advance. Get permission and avoid risking time, money, or reputation due to adverse publicity.

On the other hand, say you developed American Incense. The success of gimmick items often depends on the novelty of their instructions. Should you try to copyright the directions? How effective is the protection?

As with patents, a lawsuit is necessary to enforce your rights against an infringer. Unlike patents, copyrights are quick and inexpensive to obtain. Copyrighting something will discourage copying, so it is worth the minimal effort it takes. It can be easily done without an attorney. No search is necessary to determine whether the work is similar to existing copyrighted material.

Not everything can be copyrighted. The law protects "original works of authorship" fixed in tangible form. Those especially relevant for new product development include:

- Labels

- Instruction manuals

- Photographs

- Computer software

- Books

- Graphic designs

- Written promotional material

- Sound recordings

- Product summaries

- Presentations

- Market analyses

Names, familiar symbols, slogans, short phrases, methods, systems, and some other types of subject matter cannot be copyrighted. Standard items such as calendars and rulers with no original authorship are not copyrightable.

A copyright grants the exclusive right to reproduce, revise, distribute, display, or sell the material. Ideas are not protected. Only the precise way in which an idea is expressed can be copyrighted. Mere ownership of, say, an original painting does not give one the right to copy it to make greeting cards. The owner of the painting can sell it, but cannot reproduce the images in it without the copyright owner's permission.

Likewise, a written description of a machine can be copyrighted. This would prevent others from copying the *description*, but nothing can keep them from describing the same idea in their own words. Nor would it prevent them from making, using, or selling the machine itself. Only a patent would accomplish that.

Every work is automatically copyrighted when it is created, or put into fixed form. However, to preserve the right, all published copies must carry in an obvious place all of the following elements of a copyright notice:

- A copyright symbol "©," the word "Copyright," *or* the abbreviation "Copr."

- The year of first publication

- The author's name or a recognizable abbreviation

If a work is "published" without any of these elements, the copyright protection is usually lost forever. The concept of publication does not require formal typesetting and printing. Rather, it has to do with dissemination of the work to other people. It is best to use the copyright notice from the outset so there will never be a question of whether a work was published without it.

For a nominal fee, you can register the copyright with the Register of Copyrights. Different types of "writing" are treated somewhat differently and require the use of different application forms. Although registration is normally not required for valid protection, it does give notice of the claim and confer certain advantages in infringement suits.

In general, for works created after January 1, 1978, when a new law went into effect, the copyright lasts for the life of the author, plus fifty years. The duration of protection for other works depends on the date of their original copyright. These matters are explained in *General Information Concerning Copyrights, Copyright Basics,* and *Duration of Copyright,* all available from the Copyright Office, Library of Congress, Washington, D. C. 20559.

There is no international copyright protection, but the United States is a member of the Universal Copyright Convention, which provides protection to nationals of member countries if certain formalities are met. For details about foreign protection, write the Copyright Office for *Circular 38a.*

Unlike a patent, a copyright is quick and easy to obtain. A copyright notice will discourage others from copying. Since it costs so little in time and money, it is foolish not to preserve a copyright whenever applicable.

Trademarks and Service Marks

A trademark is a word, name, symbol, device, or a combination of these actually used in trade with goods to indicate their source and to distinguish them from products of others. A service mark serves a similar function for services. They are essentially brand names.

The primary purposes of these marks are to indicate origin, imply quality, and stimulate demand. While they keep others from using similar names, they don't prevent them from making or selling similar goods or services.

Only the owners of the marks are entitled to use them. If your idea is a marketing concept that depends on a particular name, you had better learn at the outset whether you are free to adopt it. One of the authors of this book spent considerable time and money developing the "French Kiss" candy idea before checking the status of the name. Last-minute research

150

revealed it to be a registered trademark of a California company. The mark was not currently being used, and the company could have been contacted about licensing its use. However, it was decided that the profit potential was not great enough to pay licensing fees, and the project was abandoned with some egg on face but with tongue still safely in cheek.

To avoid a similar fiasco, you can do your own preliminary search in the *Trademark Register of the United States,* available at most libraries. Finding a registered mark in this way will save the few hundred dollars a professional search will cost. More complete searches can be done at the Patent and Trademark Office in Arlington or in the various Depository Libraries. There is a computer database in some to facilitate searches. Copies of individual registration files are available for a fee.

Marks that are actually used in interstate or foreign commerce may be registered with the Patent and Trademark Office for use with specified categories of goods. There is a Principal Register, which, among other things, raises certain presumptions that you own the mark and have the right to use it. There is also a less advantageous Supplemental Register.

The requirements for registration are quite technical and complicated. You can file your own application, but, as with patents, it is wise to consult an agent or attorney. A trademark cannot be registered if it is:

- Immoral or deceptive

- Disparaging of living or dead persons, institutions, national symbols, or beliefs

- The flag or coat of arms of any state or nation

- The name, portrait, or signature of a living person without his consent

- The name, signature, or portrait of a deceased United States President while his widow is alive, without her consent

151

- So similar to an existing mark as to cause confusion, mistake, or deception, *or*

- A common English term, common name, or a descriptive or generic term.

Mark applications are examined by the Patent and Trademark Office. After a mark is registered on the Principal Register, it is published in the *Trademark Official Gazette*, and anyone who believes he would be damaged by the registration has thirty days in which to object. This objection procedure does not apply to marks that are registered only on the Supplemental Register.

Registering a trademark or service mark grants the right and the obligation to use the circled "r" or "s" symbols or certain phrases indicating registered status. The "TM" or "SM" symbols indicate a trademark or service mark registration has been applied for but not yet granted. Use of the "registered" symbols before registration is granted is improper and may result in the denial of an application.

A mark owner has an obligation to protest its misuse or risk losing it. If a mark falls into general public use to denote a *type* of article, as opposed to a particular brand, it may be deemed generic and the trademark protection lost. Anyone making that type of article could then use the former trademark to describe it. Preventing this can require diligence in informing the public that the mark should only be used to refer to the specific brand. Former trademarks that have become generic include aspirin, cellophane, and linoleum.

Registration is effective for twenty years and is renewable, but an affidavit must be filed within six years showing that the mark is still in use and that there is no intention of abandoning it. Fees for the original registration and renewals are several hundred dollars.

Trademarks should not be confused with trade *names*. Trademarks and service marks refer to goods and services, while trade names relate to those who produce and sell them. Businesses always have trade names, but they might not use any marks. Trade names are not protected by federal law, but state law may protect them by statute or by common law concepts of unfair competition. A trade name can be registered and used as a trademark. It is then protected by the same procedures and to the same extent as any other trademark. Coca Cola is a trade name. It is also a trademark.

For detailed information on trademarks, see *General Information Concerning Trademarks* and *Trademark Rules of Practice with Forms and Statutes,* available from the Patent and Trademark Office, and other publications listed in the Resource Guide at the end of the book.

As with patents, marks are better in theory than in practice, at least for individuals and small businesses. They are difficult to obtain and can be quite costly to maintain and protect. On the other hand, if you have ample financial resources, the system can be most effective. Inadvertently running afoul of someone with a mark and the means to enforce it can be costly indeed.

One of the authors helped found a small company that sold mushroom salad dressing, using a red and white check pattern for the border on its label. Although this very common pattern was used solely to achieve an attractive design, the firm was promptly "requested" by attorneys from the Ralston Purina Company to remove it. Even though they believed the *border* design did not in any way infringe the Ralston trademarked checkerboard *square,* the producers of the mushroom-flavored dressing had to comply. Doing battle with the enormous, multi-billion-dollar Ralston Purina was out of the question, and the cost of revising all of the graphics and printing new labels was more than enough to put the fledgling salad dressing manufacturers out of business.

State and Common Law Protections

Patents, copyrights, and trademarks are all created by federal law. Individual states may afford additional protection under such common law concepts as "unfair competition" and "trade secrets." Although the laws of each state differ, they all follow a similar pattern. The following discussion assumes a product that is not patented.

Trade Secrets

Say you have a special formula for SUPERCOLA which makes it taste better than Coke, with its own secret recipe, Pepsi, Like, Royal Crown, Shasta, or any of the other colas currently on the market. This is a trade secret.

A trade secret is basically confidential information used in a business to give a competitive advantage over others who do not know or use it. It can include formulas, patterns, customer lists, manufacturing processes, devices, and many other types of information, including new product ideas.

You can own a trade secret even if you are not in business, as long as it is of economic value and is confidential. In deciding whether something is a trade secret, courts look at how well known it is, how valuable it is, the effort taken by the owner to protect it, and how difficult it was to develop.

Common law trade secret protection differs significantly from patent law:

- There is no obligation to disclose the details publicly. In fact, while confidential disclosures do not destroy the protection, indiscriminate or unconditional ones do. If selling or exhibiting your product reveals the secret, you may no longer be protected. The same is probably true if you enter your idea in a contest.

- There is no arbitrary time limitation on common law protection, as there is with patents.

- The rigid standards for patentability do not apply to common law.

- Common law does *not* bestow the right to exclude others from making and selling an identical product if they legitimately have information that enables them to do so. The crucial question is basically *how* they got that information. Unless they obtained it wrongfully, they can use it any way they wish. Therefore, to maintain your protection, you must take precautions to ensure that your idea remains confidential. If another individual independently invents your product, however, you have no rights against him.

How does someone "wrongfully" obtain a trade secret? It can happen in any number of ways. Theft and industrial espionage certainly fit the category. But so does breach of a "confidential relationship," a term that essentially encompasses any situation where the parties anticipate that information will be kept confidential or used only with permission. This can arise from an express written agreement, or it may be implied from the circumstances.

For example, when you submit an idea to a company, the law presumes that you are doing so with the expectation of payment. The company may not use the concept without compensating you. Most firms will agree to review your idea only if you sign a document disclaiming a confidential relationship. They do this not to steal your ideas, but to protect themselves from unjust lawsuits by disgruntled inventors.

One precaution you can take is to tell people you are dealing with that the information is confidential and should not be disclosed. You could try to have them sign a simple form stating they will respect your confidence. Ideally, everyone should sign, including consultants, employees, suppliers, manufacturers, graphic artists, and anyone else to whom you must reveal the information. In reality, asking people to sign such an agreement will usually alienate them and destroy trust.

About the only time these agreements are recommended is for presenting ideas to small companies. A sample can be found in the Resource Guide. Informal requests, handshakes, and eye contact are probably more effective in most situations.

Unfair Competition

The state common law equivalent of federally registered trademarks is the doctrine of unfair competition. Through consistent use, the public often comes to associate certain words or symbols with the goods or services of a particular company. They are said to have acquired a "secondary meaning." For example, most people will immediately think of McDonald's when they see golden arches. Even if this were not a registered trademark, it would probably be protected by the common law of unfair competition.

This law basically prohibits anyone else from "passing off" or "palming off" his goods or services as those of a competitor by using the words and symbols associated with the competitor. Therefore, you probably could not franchise fast foods under similar yellow spans without hearing from McDonald's lawyers. Similarly, you could not market canned peas using a laughing leafy leviathan logo. Geographic designations, common words, and even your own name may acquire secondary meaning relating to others' products. If that is the case, you cannot use them in ways that would tend to confuse your goods with theirs. If your name is Husch, for example, you would probably be ill advised to call your new footwear "Husch Puppies" even if you clearly disavow any connection with Wolverine Worldwide and its Hush Puppies. This is a technical area of the law, and if you have any doubts, consult a knowledgeable attorney.

Summary

Many legal rights and considerations will be of concern for developing a concept. Often several rights apply to different aspects of the same product. For full protection, it is necessary to know which are appropriate and how and when they are applicable. It is also important to decide whether the protection afforded is worth the time and money required to get it. Patent and trademark rights are not only expensive to obtain, but are costly to preserve. Copyright, on the other hand, is quick and easy to get, and it should be obtained whenever possible. State rights vary. Their protections are not difficult to obtain.

Finally, whatever the protection for your own product, also be aware of any potential infringement of the rights of others. Protect your ideas from others as others protect their ideas from you.

CHAPTER 9: PRESENTING IDEAS FOR SALE

The *GoochyGoo* Chronicles

How totally frustrating! I fly all the way to New York to see the guy in charge of new products. I have a definite, confirmed appointment. And he isn't in. "What kind of a company is this?" At least his secretary is friendly . . . . . "What? You doubt if he'll be back in today? How long have you been this guy's secretary? He does this all the time? You think I'd be better off going to see Procter & Gamble in Cincinnati? What a thing to say. You sure don't have much company loyalty, do you? Why should you? They're all terrible here? How about another company that's a little closer? Warner Lambert, huh? In New Jersey? How much do you think a cab would cost?" . . . . . Seventy-five bucks. That sure wasn't worth it. Barely made my flight. I'm glad to be heading back to California. The people in these big companies are dead. Totally unreceptive to any outside ideas. I can remember his exact words: "That's the best presentation we've ever seen from an individual. It's a great concept, and seems to be selling sensationally. I don't think we're interested at the present time." I guess I do battle with Gucci on my own. Gucci versus Goochy . . . . . Maybe Rick was right. I should have found someone I know at those huge companies. A

157

contact to go through. Live and learn . . . . . ♫ ♪ *California,*
here I come, dum dedumdum, dum dum dum . . . . . ♪♪♪♫

Selling a new product idea or invention is not easy. It is extremely challenging. It takes time, energy, and money. It can be frustrating, disillusioning, and discouraging. It is often impossible to talk with companies because they believe they have thought of everything already and they are afraid of being sued.

Nevertheless, this path is still worth pursuing. It is high adventure, and when you succeed, it is like having a baby, making a hole-in-one, saving a life, getting religion, or winning the Nobel Prize. It can be a peak experience of the first magnitude.

Finding a Company to Buy Your Idea

Just as you targeted the ultimate consumers for your new product or service, you must research the best potential corporate buyers for your concept. This involves evaluating its suitability for specific firms, obtaining the names of key decision-makers, and tailoring presentations to appeal to their needs and capabilities. Far from being tedious, this research is fascinating and easy to do. There are several approaches to undertake simultaneously.

Go back to the stores and look again at the shelves. This need not be a full marathon. Sprints and dashes are more appropriate at this time. Almost every package gives the name and location of its producer. Sometimes this information is in small print or in an obscure place on the label. Look for products compatible with yours. For example, if your product is a kitchen gadget, note manufacturers of all types of kitchen wares. Do not just consider those with similar products, as most firms want to extend their present lines into new areas. In addition, companies in completely unrelated fields may be interested in your idea as part of a "tie-in" or premium to promote purchase of their existing merchandise.

Suppose your new product is The Great Pet Tender. You might decide to make it function like a telephone answering machine, so an owner could call home and talk to Fido, or Tabby, or Polly whenever the urge hit. This is a rather complex item to make and sell, so you will want to look for companies in the pet field and in the recording and answering machine fields. Perhaps you can engineer a joint venture with a company from each area. The answering machine maker would produce The Great Pet Tender, and the pet people would market it. Get the names of prospective companies from existing merchandise.

Go back to the library and look in the relevant reference books for names of additional prospects. You are already familiar with many of these sources. Now you will want to dig deeply into specific ones to learn as much as possible about each company you plan to contact:

- The *Thomas Register of American Manufacturers* is essentially a national Yellow Pages, giving names, addresses, and pertinent information for thousands of firms. The listings are organized by product category as well as company name.

- Dun & Bradstreet's *Reference Book of Corporate Managements* gives detailed biographical data for some seventy-five thousand principal officers of twelve thousand leading companies. It supplies name, title, year of birth, marital status, degrees and schools attended, military service, employment history, and other vital statistics.

- Standard & Poor's *Register of Corporations, Directors and Executives* lists forty-five thousand corporations with addresses and telephone numbers, division names, and annual sales, as well as names, titles, functions, and detailed personal data on approximately 450,000 company executives.

• The *Million Dollar Directory* and the *Middle Market Directory*, both from Dun & Bradstreet, contain information on tens of thousands of businesses with net worths over $1 million and between $500,000 and $1 million, respectively.

• The additional invaluable references include *MacRae's Blue Book, Moody's Industrial Manual, Sweet's Catalog File,* and others listed in the Resource Guide. They all contain a wealth of information.

Write to company treasurers for free copies of the annual reports. These will provide additional information on current earnings, divisions, officers, and much more.

Go back to the trade journals and concentrate on the manufacturers and their products. Get a feel for which companies are moving into new areas of potential interest to you or which are most innovative overall. Most trade publications will provide annual "buyers' guides" that contain alphabetical listings of products and manufacturers.

Read the financial journals, such as *Barron's, Business Week, Forbes, Fortune,* and *The Wall Street Journal.* Browse through them generally, reading ads and articles that are relevant to the companies you have noted in your prior research, confirming what you have learned from other sources. Check the guides to periodical and business literature for articles about target companies, similar products, and consumer trends.

Distributors can be good sources of information. They know which firms are receptive to new ideas. Contact those middlemen you found helpful, update them on your progress, and ask for recommendations.

If any of "your" companies are local, visit them. Look them over. Get used to being in this setting. Check out the trade journals in the lobby. Tear out the free information and subscription cards and mail them in later to receive complimentary subscriptions. Watch the people as they go to work. Walk around to the extent you are comfortable and are permitted to do so. What kind of "feel" does this place have?

Such a visit will help reduce your nervousness later when you return on business.

Review all the information you have gathered and select the most likely prospects. The number may be five, or it may be fifty. Use common sense. All things being equal, select those with experience in *marketing* similar products as opposed to those mainly adept at *manufacturing*. The former will have established advertising and distribution structures and will probably be better able to appreciate your product's commercial worth. Do not limit yourself geographically. Your initial contacts will be by phone and mail. If you get a positive response, the investment in long distance telephoning and traveling for a presentation could pay off quite nicely.

Intrapreneuring

Perhaps your current employer is the ideal company to develop your idea. A great idea can change you from a company person into your own boss, from employee to entrepreneur. An "intrapreneur" is an entrepreneur inside a company. He or she is an ambitious employee who creates and develops a new product or service from within an existing firm.

Companies of all sizes are embracing intrapreneuring as a way to keep talented employees with pet projects from leaving to go into business for themselves. It also has proven to be quite profitable for the firms.

In essence, the company provides financial, technical, and other assistance and gets ownership of the product and profits in return. The enterprising employee can be compensated in a number of ways, often with some form of incentive bonus or, occasionally, a little equity ownership in the new venture.

As an employee, you have the advantage of judging the appropriateness of your idea for a company you already know and where you have contacts. You can evaluate with an insider's eye whether your product would be consistent with existing marketing and distribution structures. Or perhaps you have an idea that the company could put to use in its internal operations—in the office or assembly line, for example.

Entrepreneurial abilities are not passed out once and for all at birth as some books and articles claim. They can emerge at any time. You can even control the process. The basic ingredients for success are communication skills, conscious curiousity, self-confidence, and common sense.

Nevertheless, intrapreneuring is not for everyone. Although the practice is becoming well publicized and is supported by many large companies, not all accept it. You may have to overcome much resistance in a traditional, hierarchy-laden corporation. You might have to battle to operate in areas that are not formally open to you. You must be able and willing to cross organizational lines and take on any relevant task, no matter how lowly or mundane, that will help the venture succeed.

You must be willing to take risks, to make a personal commitment, and to devote substantial time and energy outside normal working hours. In addition, you must accept the risk of becoming an outsider to corporate culture, especially if the firm does not value independence, "irrational" devotion to a project, or unorthodox working methods.

If you are interested in pursuing intrapreneuring in more depth, there are good books and articles on the subject. They contain educational and entertaining case studies, examine technical guidelines and methods, and explore the viewpoints of both companies and intrapreneurs.

Most states have laws governing the inventions of employees. Find out where you stand legally before presenting your idea to your employer. To encourage individuals to exercise their creativity, the rights to an invention normally belong to the person who conceptualized it, unless there is a contract to the contrary. Many companies, particularly those heavily into research and development, require workers to sign such documents when they begin employment.

These contracts generally provide that all inventions made by employees during, and for a limited period after leaving, employment belong to the employer. Find out if you signed this kind of agreement and, if so, read it. Even if you signed nothing formal, such a contract may be implied if you were hired specifically to perform research and development. There have been a number of lawsuits between companies and ex-employees who began businesses with alleged proprietary information or ideas supposedly developed during the course of employment.

Even without a contract, an employer may have "shop rights," the royalty-free perogative to use an employee's invention if it was made on company time with the employer's materials and equipment. Although a few states have statutes to the contrary, the invention usually need not relate to the employment in order for shop rights to arise. Shop rights may continue to exist even after an employee leaves. To avoid them, you would probably have to do all work on your idea on your own time and in other facilities, and maintain records to prove it.

If you and your company are interested in intrapreneuring, you, of course, have no objection to your employer's using your idea. The company wants to keep you as an employee and will reward you for your creativity, energy, and talent.

You may already have been working on your project within a company, so certain people within the organization are aware of it. Get and use their support. See if you can warm them up to the project before you make a formal presentation. Approaching companies other than your current employer is discussed in the following section.

Initial Contact with the Company

Most companies have established structures for generating and developing new product ideas. They are called new business divisions, research and development groups, new product departments, innovation committees, product planning sections, and so on. Strange as it may seem, it is almost always disadvantageous to contact or submit anything to anyone in these divisions. Often their major function is to act as a screen or filter to prevent outside ideas from getting in.

If you do get them to listen to a great idea, they may keep it from being reviewed by their superiors just because they didn't think of it themselves. If you then try to go over their heads and personally escort your idea up the corporate ladder, you will become engrossed in a frustrating and fruitless endeavor. Your creative energies will evaporate or turn to anger.

Some people may advise you to present your concept to a company's outside advertising agency. This is not an avenue worth pursuing. While advertising people are sometimes creative and have novel marketing ideas, they usually do not have any authority to review concepts on behalf of client companies. Also, they rarely entertain the notion that anyone outside their own agency might have ideas worth listening to. The people you need to address are those within the company whose job it is to make decisions at the highest level.

Likewise, do not submit an idea to any technical department within a company. Engineers and technicians rarely have much decision-making power. They usually know little about marketing and will see only the specialized problems with your concept. You will not want to reveal much technical information in your first contacts anyway.

Always attempt to deal with executives who will recognize the worth of your ideas and will not be concerned with appropriating them for their own use. It is usually best to write directly to the president. He or she will personally route your inquiry to the right people, and you are then most likely to receive proper treatment.

Now you are ready to make contact. First, a word about how *not* to do it. Here is an example of the many thousands of amateurish letters received by companies each year:

New Product Department
The Universal Gismo Company
1234 Conglomerate Circle
Everytown, Anystate Zip

Ladies/Gentlemen:

Please send me information on how I may submit an idea for a new product to your company.

Sincerely,

A much better approach is a personal letter directed to the president or chief executive officer. These people are not on top by chance. They will know just what to do with a good idea when they see one. Your letter should be flawlessly professional. It must grab their attention instantly. They will devote no more than a few seconds to it before putting it into their own follow-up file or their secretaries' send-the-no-thank-you-form file.

Type it on your personal letterhead. If you do not have any, get some printed or make it yourself at the local copy shop. Use top quality lettering and high-grade bond paper. Here is a sample of the kind of letter to send:

Ms. Ima Topdog
President
General Standard Widget, Inc.
4321 New Product Plaza
Downtown, Bigstate Zip

Dear Ms. Topdog:

I have a new product innovation which will let your company come out with a significant extension for your existing widget line. It is fully consistent with your present business and lines of distribution.

It should require only modest capital investment, yet the innovative nature of the concept will permit a stand-alone brand that promises substantial profit.

Since new product concepts are difficult to protect, I am unwilling to submit it through the mail. Rather, I request only fifteen minutes with you or someone else with sufficient marketing background and position in the company to act with authority.

Please call or write so that we may arrange such a meeting at your office or mine at your convenience. I am enclosing a brief résumé so that you will know something about my business qualifications.

Sincerely,

A letter such as this is your best bet for a prompt response. Sometimes that will be a personal phone call. Tailor your correspondence to the particular circumstances. If you have applied for or obtained a patent, mention that fact.

If you have not received any response after a couple of weeks, follow up with a telephone call to the president. Mention your letter and ask for an appointment. If you can't get past the secretary, send a follow-up letter in which you mention your first letter and ask for an appointment. Persistence pays off.

Having an "in" to get an audience with a company executive can be extremely helpful. Any type of contact can be useful—old school friends, work acquaintances, your uncle's cousin, frat buddies, sorority sisters, friends of friends, the couple you met in the Bahamas last year, or the guy you sat next to at the ball game last Saturday. This is "networking" in action. No matter how tenuous the contact, it can open doors.

Personal connections can cut through miles of red tape and corporate sluggishness and help ease executives' fears of legal problems involved in evaluating outside ideas. Although your contacts may not be able to introduce you to the president, they can supply intimate information about internal company affairs that could prove invaluable.

Response to Expect from Companies

Management is usually quite concerned over the legal problems associated with unsolicited ideas. Because of the possibility of someone unjustly claiming misappropriation of a trade secret, most firms are extremely reluctant to consider product ideas from external sources. Therefore, you may receive a letter requesting a signed submission agreement and waiver of confidentiality.

As noted in the last chapter, receiving information without an accompanying disclaimer of compensation can create a confidential relationship. This would require the company to maintain secrecy and refrain from using the concept without your permission.

Misunderstandings can easily arise. If a company is already working on a new product, it would not want to pay an outsider for the same idea. An inventor who does not know about such prior research and development might see a company successfully introduce "his" product several months after his submission. If he thought it was derived from his idea, he might assume it was stolen and bring a lawsuit. Even if both parties were acting in good faith, there is still a messy dispute to be resolved.

The expense and adverse publicity generated by even unjustified suits are problems most companies wish to avoid. They would rather not have to go to court to prove they created products on their own. After all, they have their own R & D and product planning departments, and they have truly thought of just about everything. They consider most of the ideas and suggestions they receive in the mail to be either a total waste of time or lawsuits looking for places to happen. As a result, some companies often refuse to look at *any* unsolicited ideas whatsoever. They will send you a polite form letter stating their policy, and that will be the end of your correspondence.

Most firms have not adopted such strict policies, but still have procedures to protect themselves. Some simply refuse to look at any ideas that are not patented. Others require you to waive all claims of secrecy and rights to remuneration before they will review your concept. Business journals advise companies to return all unsolicited submissions unread or route them directly to their legal departments for safekeeping, still unread, until they have received signed waiver agreements.

These submission agreements provide that you are voluntarily disclosing your idea without solicitation and with no expectation of confidentiality. They further state that although the company may allow you to present your idea, it has no obligation to use it or to pay you if it does and that you will make no claim for compensation except pursuant to a formal, written contract. These forms may also stipulate that your only protection is through the patent laws. A simplified sample of the many variations you might be asked to sign appears at the end of the Resource Guide.

Most large companies will not even look at your idea until they have received an executed agreement such as this. Then they may or may not evaluate it. They may tell you they are already working on something similar. They will probably send you back a form letter stating that they are not interested. They will probably not return your materials, so you will have to write and ask them to do so. They may not do anything at all. Don't be discouraged. Write to another prospect.

Not all companies are this cautious, and many firms fail to follow their own procedures. But if you are asked to sign one of these forms, you will have to do so if you want your concept considered. Even if you have an inside contact, he or she may have to make you sign such an agreement before listening to you. Don't worry. The forms are primarily to filter out crackpots and protect the company from "inventors" looking for cheap lawsuits. If the company likes your idea, it will usually deal openly and honestly with you. To repeat, *the critical thing is to get the right person to look at it.*

Submitting Ideas to Government Agencies

Government agencies can be approached with products and ideas that relate to their activities. Contact them for their policies and procedures. As with private firms, you will usually be required to sign a submission agreement.

Say you have the idea for a method by which cities could improve their collections on parking tickets. They would enter all paid citations in a lottery as an incentive for payment. Drawings and sweepstakes are becoming increasingly popular and, if not illegal in your state, you believe local governments might welcome the concept. You evaluate the idea as you would any other, research any relevant legal considerations, and offer it to your town in exchange for appropriate compensation. Your chances of making a sale are probably better than winning in a lottery.

The Presentation

What makes a successful presentation? You cannot just walk into a corporation's headquarters and ask to see the president or the upper-echelon executive in charge of new products. Getting an audience results from the networking and letter-writing process described above.

You may be asked to submit your materials in writing or in person. In either case, present everything concisely and professionally. How you package your idea is as important as the idea itself. You can use slide shows and videos, attractive models, bells and whistles, dogs and ponies, or a complete three-ring circus. Or you can be low-keyed and discreet.

For written material use a high-quality binder with each page enclosed in a clear plastic sheet-protector. Begin with an attention-grabber, a captivating picture of the product, or striking package design. Nothing should look funky or too homemade. If you do not trust your judgment or abilities, it is worth the expense to hire a design expert.

Your presentation should be specially tailored for each company and cover all major concerns, especially ease of manufacture, means of distribution, and projected consumer demand. Do not include suggestions about appropriate compensation for you. If the company is interested in your idea, it will open the negotiations. Never tell a company how eager its competitors will be to see your idea. Such amateurism and hollow threats will immediately ruin your credibility and chances for success. Be calm and cool. Let them get excited.

What are the company's concerns? They basically boil down to one question: Will it make an acceptable profit? Everything in your presentation must in some way be directed to that bottom line.

The following is a general checklist for topics to cover. The essentials will vary for different companies and types of product. Use common sense when deciding what to include, and don't overdo it. Having too much is worse than having too little.

- Describe the demand for the product. State clearly who will buy the product, how many will be purchased, and at what price. Highlight the results of your market research and testing. Include statistics from industry magazines, trade associations, government sources, and your investigation into present and projected consumption of similar products.

- Identify and emphasize the benefits to consumers.

- Discuss all practicable applications. Perhaps your concept is for an automatic stirring device that utilizes a rotating magnet beneath a container and a separate metal mixer inside. Your main idea and prototype are for a gourmet kitchen item. But point out that your "Magic Mixer" also has great potential for restaurants, wineries, breweries, school cafeterias, and many other food processing applications.

- Outline the start-up expenses and production costs. You should have them well-refined by this time. Set forth your assumptions and sources of information. A smaller company must be financially able to withstand the period of product development.

- Demonstrate how your idea fits in the company's present product mix and is compatible with existing distribution systems. Or show how it is a logical extension through some meaningful connection, such as compatibility of manufacturing. Your aim is to show that the firm's existing resources can efficiently handle the product without major changes in financing, manpower, or management.

- Make sure the product fits the company's image. Suppose you want to sell the "Freudian Slips" concept and have found the perfect lingerie manufacturer, but you are afraid the idea may be too suggestive. Can you change it slightly to make it acceptable? Perhaps you should look for less conservative firms that might be more amenable to the idea.

- Describe the competition, if any, and how your product will fit into the picture. Explain how it will be positioned to penetrate the market and succeed over existing and potential competitors.

- Discuss the relevant legal considerations, such as potential patents, trademarks, or copyrights. Describe what you have already done for protection. If you have applied for, but not yet obtained, a patent, you can submit a copy of the application to the company, but it is best *not* to include copies of the claims, filing number, or filing date of the patent application.

- Cover the relevant safety considerations.

- A prototype can make or break a presentation. A good working model is usually essential to demonstrate both the uniqueness of an idea and the fact that it can be made into a real product.

- Present financial projections and pricing strategies for a successful roll-out. Will a high price risk attracting competition? Is it wiser keep the price low from the start and try to corner the market? Don't overdo the details here, as your figures could be routed to some eager young MBA who will find your analysis unsophisticated or reject it on the basis of form rather than content. If a company is interested, it will do its own detailed analysis.

- Finally, include your résumé and references. Emphasize your business background and any new product successes you may have had. Be brief. And don't fake it.

All relevant items should be covered. Have alternate approaches ready. Cover all angles. But don't use research as a means of procrastination. Make a date for a presentation.

Corporate executives view their time as extraordinarily valuable and limited. Thus, your presentation must be concise and well-organized. Try to fine-tune it so that you can cover everything within fifteen minutes. It should only extend beyond that time as a result of questions and comments from your audience.

Bring everything you will need, including extra batteries, extension cords, and any props or accessories, no matter how common. Never rely on the availability of anything. Do everything possible to make the presentation smooth. At the very least, being prepared will avoid delays. You certainly do not want to spend your limited meeting time waiting for someone to scout around for the company slide projector. You will maintain a high level of believability if you are completely organized.

Rehearse at home before family and friends. Get their feedback. Decide on the best order for presenting your materials and the right point for unveiling your prototype. Practice. Find out what works best. Make sure your slides aren't in the tray upside down.

Your presentation may be to one person or a number of people. Try to set up with your audience facing you from one direction so you can maintain eye contact with everyone. Pay attention to each person present. Incidentally, if you are asked something you don't know during a presentation, the best answer is, "I don't know. I will find out and get back to you." Don't try to bluff these people. This is not a poker game. They are experts. Besides, this follow-up will provide a legitimate excuse for further contact.

The most important thing to do is listen. If your audience starts talking, let them talk. It is a good signal that they are interested. You will be tempted to interrupt and tell them all the fine points. Don't do it. Just listen. They know their business better than you, and if your product is right for them, they will know it.

What if they want you to leave your materials so they may be reviewed in greater detail? Do so without hesitation.

Presentation of your idea includes presentation of yourself. Image is very important. Like most of us, corporate executives are more comfortable when dealing with people similar to themselves. This does not mean that your product will be accepted if you wear the right suit. But, wearing the *wrong* suit can subtly affect your reception. You may want to consult one of the many books on unwritten dress codes and corporate behavior, or try the following experiment:

> Go to the lobby of a large office building, if posssible one containing a potential target company. Observe how individuals dress and act. Ride the elevators to the top a few times. Note the appearance of people who get off at each floor. You will perceive patterns that indicate the various dress codes observed at different companies.

This is mainly for large companies. For smaller firms, where the president may be in overalls out in the shop, you will want to dress more informally. In any case, use common sense and be yourself as much as possible. You needn't sell your soul or compromise your identity. Just look sharp and be as honest and knowledgable as you can. Consider this your shot at the Olympics. You would not try the high jump in high heels, nor would you enter a gymnastics event wearing skis and grand slalom garb.

Other requirements for professionalism are punctuality, a firm handshake, and a relaxed ability to look people in the eye. Smile and be friendly, but not jovial or flip. For some, the presentation—the face-to-face confrontation with their ideas on the line—is the most exciting stage of the entire process. To others, it is the ultimate in anxiety. You need never feel intimidated. Even the largest company is comprised of mere humans. The worst that can happen is rejection of your idea. That is their loss, not your failure, and it is certainly not to be feared.

If your idea is turned down, try to find out why. It will help you determine whether something needs to be changed or whether you should try another type of company.

On occasion, someone in a company will take you aside and propose that you go into business together to develop the product. He or she will provide the expertise and contacts; you will provide the idea and energy. You will both put up capital.

173

Usually the insider will want keep his job, at least part-time, while you do the lion's share of the work. Deals such as this can succeed, but they are shaky. It may be wise to clear the matter with the company before beginning such a venture.

In considering such a proposal, ask yourself: "Why doesn't this person quit and work full-time with me? Why am I considering reversing my decision to sell the idea rather than go into business? If this employee thinks my concept is so good, why doesn't he take it straight to the president? Is he being disloyal to his present employer by not taking a great idea to the top? If so, will he be disloyal to me?" On the other hand, if he or she is interested and believes in the project after the company has rejected it, you may have a partner. In any case, go very slowly in this situation.

Compensation

If a company wants to buy your idea, what sort of a deal can you expect to make? The two basic options are to sell outright or negotiate a royalty agreement.

Selling the idea outright, or "assigning" it, means getting a fixed sum for complete transfer of all rights to the product and any spin-offs and extensions. Outright sales are simpler than royalty deals. However, if the product becomes a hit, you will not participate in the bonanza. While you may get some positive strokes from being known as the creator, they will be balanced by the negative punches of knowing you sold out for a song and are missing the big payoffs.

These considerations will be of far more immediate significance to you than to others. Friends and relatives will think it fabulous that you have something on the shelves, and they will not care much about whether you received maximum return. And they are probably right. The main thing is to get an idea out there. This will enhance your credibility for future endeavors as new product guru. Try to remember these things when you are weeping inside about missing out on the jackpot.

Royalty, or licensing, arrangements are more common and usually more desirable than outright sales. A license is a transfer of less than all the rights; some are reserved. These can include limitations on time, territory, and other aspects. Licensing usually means that you grant specified rights in exchange for percentage payments based on an agreed formula. There are many possible variations.

An "exclusive" license means you agree not to grant the use to anyone else for a stated period or territory, *and* you agree not to use the product or process yourself. In contrast, "nonexclusive" licenses allow you to grant rights to additional licensees or to use them yourself. Nonexclusive licenses can protect you from licensees who do not generate adequate sales and royalties. Exclusive licenses are more valuable, so the royalty percentage is usually higher. Variations are possible in which the license is exclusive for a stated time and then becomes nonexclusive, or it is exclusive unless it is not developed within a certain time, and so on.

Sometimes a company will want an option on your idea. It will pay you a certain amount in exchange for your not selling to anyone else for a specified period. It buys this time to consider your concept. At any point before the stated period expires, the company can exercise the option to enter into a contract with you on terms you previously accepted. It does not *have* to buy the idea. It can do nothing and let the option expire. Meanwhile your hands are tied, and other potential deals may be lost. So be wary of entering into this type of arrangement, especially for lengthy periods.

There are many ways to structure payments in licensing deals. Royalties usually will not start until sales have been made. However, it is sometimes possible to negotiate an "advance." This means that you receive a small payment before production starts. Once sales begin, your royalties are credited against the advance, and you receive no further payments until the accrued royalties equal the advance.

Licensing agreements will be for a specified percent of a defined base. It typically ranges between one and ten percent, but anything is possible. The base can be "gross" sales, often called "factory" sales, or "net" sales. It will depend on the specific industry and product involved. Gross sales are the total amounts the company receives for sales of the product. Net sales are gross sales minus cash discounts, returns, and spoilage. The base does not always relate to dollars. Royalties

175

for processes, chemicals, or components will normally be based on volume or the number of items produced.

The contract should state precisely when royalty payments are due and provide some way for you to verify sales figures. If you can negotiate it, include a contract clause that the license terminates and all rights in the invention or product revert to you if the product is not marketed within a specified time; if a specified number are not produced or sold; if a royalty payment is not timely; or if confidentiality of trade secrets is not maintained.

Your agreement should also require the company to carry sufficient product liability insurance, naming you as additional insured. It should already have such insurance, and adding your name will cost very little. It could be an invaluable asset for you, however. Inventors may face some legal exposure for defectively designed products that result in personal injury or property damage to third parties, even if the products are manufactured by others.

If you don't have a patent, what you will be licensing is a trade secret. Even if you are licensing a patent, a company may also need trade secrets from you that are not disclosed by the patent. Therefore, your agreement may be a license of both patent and trade secrets. Some attorneys recommend having separate agreements for each.

If licensing a patent, try to get the company to agree to enforce it against infringement.

Other points to consider are rights to future improvements, secrecy obligations of both parties, audits, responsibilities arising from third-party claims, duration of the agreement, and so on. Consult your attorney for help with these and other clauses that should be included.

You will probably want professional assistance, particularly near the end of negotiations. But use your lawyer advisedly. As suggested above, you may have to forego some advantages in order to make the deal. While you should carefully consider your attorney's advice, you must stay in charge and decide for yourself what is acceptable. After a transaction collapses, you will find little solace in saying that your lawyer blew it.

Contracts have to be carefully constructed to reflect clearly the terms and conditions as understood by all parties. Most firms will have their own documents. Preprinted forms are not sacred. They can be modified in any way. Likewise, if you should ever be in the position of having to draft an agreement from scratch, do not copy any forms or documents without giving each provision adequate thought with respect to your particular situation.

Although it has been said many times, *read before signing*. If something is not written the way you remember or doesn't read the way you want, rewrite it yourself. Contracts may be written in plain English. They don't have to be filled with "whereases" and "heretofores" to be binding.

A relatively simple sample licensing agreement appears at the end of the Resource Guide. Licensing terms are a bit confusing until you have been involved in negotiating an actual deal. Once you start bargaining over a favorite brainchild, the abstract terminology will take on meaning. Until then, this simple scenario should help:

~ *Susie came up with a sensational concept for clear-plastic, conch-shaped containers called "See-Shells." She contemplated sales to seaside vacationers for collecting and showcasing shells. She also considered selling already-filled versions for sad souls whose seashell searches fall short.*

~ *Sue screened the idea, made a prototype, and applied for a design patent on the conch-shaped contrivance. She thought See-Shells were such a super idea that surely all seaside visitors would select several.*

~ *Suddenly Susie faced the Big Decision. Should she sell a company the See-Shell concept or start her own business?*

~ *She sized herself up and decided she did not care to oversee any significant manufacturing and sales operations.*

177

~ *So Sue researched favorable firms. She soon found a company selling clear-plastic undersea field-guides for snorkelers. "Stupendous!" she shouted, and swiftly made contact to see if they'd sell compatible conches. They said yes, and then negotiations started.*

~ *Should Susie sell See-Shells straight-out? Or should she license for royalties? If she sells, she is free of See-Shells forever. She shuns the thought of complete separation. The company wants an exclusive license, but finally agrees to a U. S. exclusive. This means Sue may offer the concept to someone she knows on the shores of Sri Lanka.*

~ *But what about Sue? She wants to sell See-Shells from her stand on Kauai. She and the firm decide she may do so, and they sign the agreement for five years.*

~ *Sue's to get an advance of six thousand smackers, plus six percent of factory sales to be sent semi-annually.*

~ *See-Shells suffer sick sales for three seasons, so much so that Susie wished she'd sold it outright. Suddenly sales soar, but she is sent zero. So Sue sues.*

~ *Sue's suit's a success. She subsequently licenses See-Shells to seven fine firms and retires to her stand to sell See-Shells by the seashore.*

Negotiating

Negotiating effectively is an art. If you are in doubt about your expertise in this realm, there are many books on the subject. Take their advice with a grain of salt. Some advise assertiveness or intimidation, and others suggest forthright honesty. Learn to use and recognize various approaches. Practice with friends and family! The best bargainers combine sincerity and swagger, believability and bluff.

Everything is negotiable. If this is your first new product sale, it is wise to not be too hard-nosed. Make the deal, even if it is somewhat in the company's favor. Do not risk losing its interest by trying for too much. Once you have a transaction under your belt and can point to one of "your" products on the shelves, your bargaining power will increase. You will have a track record. It will be easier to get in to see people with your next idea. You have created something and sold it. You have invented a real new product. You are a success.

Summary

Selling an idea is not easy. It requires many skills and often as much creativity as getting the concept in the first place. It is always a challenge and an exciting way to learn about the world and the world of business.

You will often see one of "your" ideas hit the market while you are still working on it, or after you have abandoned it. If this depresses you, you are in the wrong game. Rather, such an experience ought to make you feel exhilarated and optimistic. After all, you thought of it, too. Its appearance as a real product confirms your creative talents. It means that you have good ideas and should soon see them on the market as new products.

Getting and developing ideas is a worthwhile endeavor at any level of expertise. At its highest, it does not cause competitive feelings and actions. Instead, it provides delight in your own creativity and admiration for the great ideas of others. The ideas are what is important, not who got them. Well, under ideal circumstances, that is!

CONCLUSION: CREATIVITY AND BUSINESS

The *Goochy Goo* Chronicles

Gucci versus Goochy. *Ha! What a fool! I'm destroyed.*
Now I know how Zorba felt when he lost everything. How
was he able to dance? For me, it hurts too much to laugh, but
I'm too old to cry. But I'm not going to mope around and go
back to my old job with my tail between my legs. No way! . .
. . . *What the heck, maybe I will dance after all. Right down*
to Hollywood. Goochy Goo is a great story. It'll make a
blockbuster movie. It's the modern Horatio Alger story and
David and Goliath rolled into one. They'll love it. I think I'll
write the screenplay myself. There's more than one way to skin
a cat. What shall I call it? Goochy Goo? *No. They'll*
probably sue me. How about Gone with the Goo? Gooing
My Way? Zorba the Goo? Goo-fight at the Oilcan Corral?
Maybe The Great Goo Robbery? *Yeah! That's it. It's a sure*
winner. Hollywood, here we come . . . . . ♪♫♪ *Thank*
heaven for little goos . . . . . ♫♪

Damn! Damn! DAMN! Hollywood. What a bummer!
Worse than a backed up sink. Worse than New York. And
now it looks like I'll have to go back to the old nine-to-five.
What a mega-bummer! No time for anything. Won't even be
able to cut the grass. It sure got out of control while I was
down in Tinsel Town. Maybe I'll just rip out the whole yard
and install Astroturf. But that stuff looks so sterile. I bet they
could sell tons of it in the suburbs if it weren't quite so uniform

181

and unnatural looking. I mean, it needs a few weeds .....
Hey! That's a great idea! Astroweeds!! I'll make a
fortune. Where are the Yellow Pages? ..... ♩♩ Astroweeds
are comin' down the track, dumdedum dum dum .....
♩♩♩♩♫♪

Creativity is an invaluable part of human existence. It brings advances in both esthetic and practical realms. For an individual, creating is engrossing and exciting. In business, it is challenging and potentially profitable. But regardless of any possible monetary reward, working with ideas is a satisfying end in itself. Using the imagination sets us free. It allows us to explore and test the limits of our world and, perhaps, expand them.

Developing and selling new product ideas is creation in action at every step, from formulating and researching concepts to making prototypes and presentations, and beyond.

There is an infinite supply of ideas in the universe. Even if you don't think of yourself as an "idea person," you can be in control of getting them. All it takes is an open mind and a willingness to practice. By simply setting aside some time for being in an unrestricted imaginative space, you can generate an unlimited number of concepts for actual products and services, promotional strategies, or anything else.

Creativity is the unifying principle in new product development. It will help you learn and recover from your mistakes. It will also keep you flexible so you can develop alternative approaches for making and selling your product or service. Sometimes the line between success and failure is simply seeing the need for a slightly different approach.

Research can be boring and monotonous, or it can be fascinating and fun. Imagination and creativity are what make the difference. The resources exist for finding out anything. Make your own rules about what information to search for and how to interpret and use it effectively.

By definition, everything in new product creation and development is new. There are no "right" ways, no one ideal approach. You must decide. This is both frightening and liberating. In this uncharted territory, let common sense be your compass.

Stretch yourself, but don't try to do everything on your own. Don't squander your precious energy, time, and capital. Know your limitations, and get help when you need it. Watch the experts and learn from them.

Getting and developing ideas is both creation and recreation. Start now and keep going. You can make a new world for yourself.

In the rush and madness of modern living, we sometimes forget where we are in the world. We accept the supermarket and Superbowl as normal, as necessities, rarely giving any thought to how thoroughly amazing such things are in the history of man, adrift on a rock in infinite space. They were once just ideas.

Great ideas are worth searching for. They engross us body and soul. Developing ideas makes us more alive and keeps us aware of our place in the universe. It reaffirms the sacredness of freedom and the joy of unlimited choice.

RESOURCE GUIDE

Do not be intimidated by the scope of this Resource Guide and the Bibliography. All of the most important information has been distilled and condensed into the preceding text. Look upon the following as a supermarket of suggestions. Cruise the columns as you would browse through the stores at the mall. See what is available should you wish to dig more deeply into a subject.

PUBLICATIONS

Advertising Age Yearbook. Annual. Chicago: Crain, 1984.

Applied Science and Technology Index. Monthly, except July, with cumulations. Bronx, New York: H. W. Wilson.

Ayer Directory of Publications. Annual. Philadelphia: Ayer Press.

Business Firms Master Index. Jennifer Mossman and Donna Wood, eds. Detroit: Gale Research, 1985.

A Business Information Guidebook. Oscar Figueroa and Charles Winkler. New York: AMACOM, 1980.

Business Information Sources. Lorna M. Daniells, Rev. ed. Berkeley: University of California Press, 1985.

Business Organizations and Agencies Directory. Anthony T. Kruzas, Kay Gill, and Robert C. Thomas, eds. 2d ed. Detroit: Gale Research, 1984.

Business Periodical Index. Monthly, except July, with cumulations. Bronx, New York: Wilson.

Business Services and Information: The Guide to the Federal Government. Timothy C. Weckesser, Joseph R. Whaley, and Miriam Whaley, eds. New York: Interscience/Wiley, 1978.

Consultants and Consulting Organizations Directory: A Reference Guide to Concerns and Individuals Engaged in Consultation for Business and Industry. Janice McLean, ed. 6th ed. Detroit: Gale Research, 1984.

Consumer Sourcebook: A Directory and Guide to Government Organizations, Information Centers, Clearinghouses, and Toll-Free Numbers, Associations, Centers, and Institutes, Media Services, Publications Relating to Consumer Topics, Sources of Recourse and

185

Resource Guide

Advisory Information, Company and Trade Names. Paul Wasserman and Gita Siegman. 4th ed. Detroit: Gale Research, 1983.

Data Sources for Business and Market Analysis. Natalie D. Frank and John V. Ganly. 3d ed. Metuchen, New Jersey: Scarecrow Press, 1983.

Directory of Business and Financial Services. Mary M. Grant and Riva Berleant-Schiller, comps. 8th ed. Special Libraries Association, 1984.

Directory of Directories. James M. Ethridge. Biennial, with supplements. Detroit: Gale Research.

A Directory of Information Resources in the United States: Federal Government. Rev. ed. Washington, D. C.: United States Library of Congress, 1974.

Editor & Publisher Market Guide. Annual. New York: Editor and Publisher Company.

Encyclopedia of Associations. Katherine Gruber, ed. 20th ed. Detroit: Gale Research, 1986.

Encyclopedia of Business Information Sources: A Detailed Listing of Primary Subjects of Interest to Managerial Personnel, with a Record of Sourcebooks, Periodicals, Organizations, Directories, Handbooks, Bibliographies and Other Sources of Information on Each Topic. Paul Wasserman, Charlotte Georgi, and James Woy, eds. 5th ed. Detroit: Gale Research, 1983.

Encyclopedia of Information Systems and Services. Anthony T. Kruzas and John Schmittroth, Jr., eds. 5th ed. Detroit: Gale Research, 1982.

Exhibits Schedule: Annual Directory of Trade and Industrial Shows. Successful Meetings Magazine, Directory Department, 633 Third Avenue, New York, New York 10017.

F & S Index of Corporations and Industries. Weekly, with cumulations. Cleveland: Predicasts.

Government Research Centers Directory: A Descriptive Guide to Government and Government-Related Research and Development Centers, Institutes, Laboratories, Test Stations, Bureaus, Offices, and Other Related Facilities. 2d ed. Anthony T. Kruzas and Kay Gill, eds. 3d ed. Detroit: Gale Research, 1982 (and supplement 1984).

Guide to American Directories. Biennial. B. Klein, ed. Coral Springs, Florida: B. Klein.

A Guide to Consumer Markets. Annual. Helen Axel, ed. New York: The Conference Board.

Resource Guide

Guide to Reference Books. Eugene P. Sheehy, ed. 9th ed., 2d supplement. Chicago: American Library Association, 1982.

How to Use the Business Library, with Sources of Business Information. Herbert Webster Johnson, Anthony J. Faria, and Ernest L. Maier. 5th ed. Cincinnati, Ohio: South-Western, 1984.

Industrial Market Information Guide. Annual. Chicago: Crain Communication.

Library Bibliographies and Indexes: A Subject Guide to Resource Material Available from Libraries, Information Centers, Library Schools, and Library Associations in the U. S. and Canada. Paul Wasserman and Esther Herman, eds. Detroit: Gale Research, 1975.

MacRae's Blue Book. Annual. Hinsdale, Illinois: Macrae's Blue Book Company.

Middle Market Directory. Annual. Parsippany, New Jersey: Dun & Bradstreet.

Million Dollar Directory. Annual. Parsippany, New Jersey: Dun & Bradstreet.

Moody's Industrial Manual. Annual, with supplements. New York: Moody's Investors Service.

National Trade and Professional Associations of the United States.

New York Times Index. Semi-monthly, with cumulations. New York: The New York Times.

Online Database Search Services Directory. Annual. John Schmittroth, Jr., and Doris Morris Maxfield, eds. Detroit: Gale Research.

Omni Online Database Directory 1985. Owens Davies and Mike Edelhart. New York: Macmillan/Collier, 1985.

Packaging Marketplace: The Practical Guide to Packaging Sources. George Hanlon, ed. Detroit: Gale Research, 1978.

Public Affairs Information Service Bulletin. Semi-monthly, with cumulations. New York: Public Affairs Information Service.

Readers' Guide to Periodical Literature. Semi-monthly, with periodic cumulations. Bronx, New York: H. W. Wilson.

Reference Book of Corporate Managements: America's Corporate Leaders. Annual. Parsippany, New Jersey: Dun & Bradstreet.

Reference Book of Manufacturers. Annual. Parsippany, New Jersey: Dun & Bradstreet.

S&MM's Survey of Buying Power. Annual. New York: *Sales and Marketing Management.*

Standard & Poor's Register of Corporations, Directors and Executives. Annual. New York: Standard & Poor's Corporation.

Standard Directory of Advertising Agencies. Three times per year. Wilmette, Illinois: National Register.
Standard Directory of Advertisers. Annual, with supplements. Wilmette, Illinois: National Register.
Standard Periodical Directory. Patricia Hagood, ed. Annual. New York: Oxbridge Communications.
Standard Rate and Data Service, Inc., Skokie, Illinois:
 Business Publication Rates and Data.
 Consumer Magazine and Farm Publication Rates and Data..
 Films for Television Rates and Data.
 Network Rates and Data.
 Newspaper Rates and Data.
 Spot Radio Rates and Data.
 Spot Television Rates and Data.
 Transit Advertising Rates and Data.
 Weekly Newspaper Rates and Data.
Statistics America: Sources for Social, Economic, and Marketing Research. Joan M. Harvey. 2d ed. Detroit: Gale Research, 1980.
Statistics Sources: A Subject Guide to Data on Industry, Business, Social, Educational, Financial, and Other Topics for the United States and Internationally. Paul Wasserman and Jacqueline O'Brien, eds. 8th ed. Detroit: Gale Research, 1983.
Surveys, Polls, Censuses, and Forecasts Directory. Detroit: Gale Research, 1983.
Sweet's Catalog File. Annual. New York: McGraw-Hill Information Systems Company.
Thomas Register Catalog File. Annual. New York: Thomas.
Thomas Register of American Manufacturers. Annual. New York: Thomas.
Trade Names Directory. Donna Wood, ed. 4th ed. Detroit: Gale Research, 1984.
Trade Shows and Professional Exhibits Directory. Robert J. Elster, Jr., ed. Detroit: Gale Research, 1985.
The Trademark Register of the United States. 20th ed. Washington, D. C.: Patent Searching Service, 1978.
Tours and Visits Directory. 2d ed. Detroit: Gale Research, 1986.
Ulrich's International Periodicals Directory. Biennial. New York: Bowker.

Resource Guide

U. S. Mail Order Shopper's Guide: A Subject Guide Listing 3,667 Unique Mail Order Catalogs. Susan Spitzer. North Hollywood, California: Wilshire Book Co., 1982.

Wall Street Journal Index. Monthly, with cumulations. New York: Dow Jones.

Where to Find Business Information: A Worldwide Guide for Everyone Who Needs the Answers to Business Questions. David M. Brownston and Gorton Carruth. 2d ed. New York: Interscience/Wiley, 1982.

Writer's Market: Where to Sell What You Write. Annual. Paula Deimling, ed. Cincinnati: Writer's Digest Books.

NEWSLETTERS AND DIRECTORIES OF NEWSLETTERS

Ayer Directory of Publications. Annual. Philadelphia: Ayer Press.

International New Product Newsletter, 6 St. James Avenue, Boston, Massachusetts 02116.

Invention Management and *Patent Newsletter*. Communications Publishing Group, 1505 Commonwealth Avenue, Boston, Massachusetts 02135.

The Lightbulb, Journal of the Inventors Workshop International, 16218 Ventura Boulevard, Encino, California 91436.

National Directory of Newsletters and Reporting Services. Robert C. Thomas, ed. 2d ed. Detroit: Gale Research, 1981.

New Product—New Business Digest. General Electric Company, Business Growth Services, 120 Erie Boulevard, Room 308, Schenectady, New York 12345.

New Product News. Dancer Fitzgerald Sample, Inc., 405 Lexington Avenue, New York, New York 10174.

Newsletter Yearbook Directory. Coral Springs, Florida: B. Klein, 1983.

Oxbridge Directory of Newsletters 1983-84. Patricia Hagood, ed. 3d rev. ed. Oxbridge Communications, Inc. 183 Madison Avenue, Suite 1108, New York, New York 10016.

Product Alert, International Product Alert, Category Reports, Lookout—Foods, and *Lookout—Nonfoods*, all offered by Marketing Intelligence Service, Ltd., 33 Academy Street, Naples, New York 14512.

Resource Guide

ASSOCIATIONS, EDUCATIONAL PROGRAMS, AND RESOURCE CENTERS

The services of and eligibility for the resources listed here vary. Write for details. Also note that the uncertainties of funding may affect their existence. This list is not intended to be exhaustive. New programs are constantly being formed. To learn of local resources, check with the Chamber of Commerce, the nearest university's business school, and professional groups.

Advanced Technology Development Center, Georgia Institute of Technology, 430 10th Street N.W., Suite N-116, Atlanta, Georgia 30332; (404) 894-3575. (Assists start-ups in high-tech industries.)

Alabama High Technology Assistance Center and Alabama Small Business Development Center, Morton Hall, University of Alabama, Huntsville, Alabama 35899; (205) 895-6407.

American Patent Law Association ("APLA"), 2001 Jefferson Davis Highway, Suite 203, Arlington, Virginia 22202; (703) 521-1680. (Publishes the *APLA Bulletin* and *Journal.*)

American Society of Inventors, c/o Engineers Club, 1317 Spruce Street, Philadelphia, Pennsylvania 19107; (215) 545-1704.

Baylor University Innovation Evaluation Program, Center for Entrepreneurship, Hankamer School of Business, Baylor University, Waco, Texas 76798; (817) 755-3766. (Provides product evaluations for a nominal fee.)

Caruth Institute of Owner-Managed Business, Cox School of Business, Southern Methodist University, Fincher Building, Room 210, Dallas, Texas 75275; (214) 692-3185.

Center for Entrepreneurial Development, Carnegie-Mellon University, 4516 Henry Street, Pittsburgh, Pennsylvania 15213; (412) 621-0700.

Center for Entrepreneurial Studies, Babson College, Babson Park, Wellesley, Massachusetts 02157; (617) 239-4332.

Center for Entrepreneurial Studies, Graduate School of Business Administration, New York University, 100 Trinity Place, New York, New York 10006; (212) 285-6150.

Center for Entrepreneurial Studies, McIntire School of Commerce, University of Virginia, Monroe Hall, Charlottesville, Virginia 22903; (804) 924-3214.

191

Resource Guide

Center for Entrepreneurship and Small Business Management, Wichita State University, 130 Clinton Hall, Box 48, Wichita, Kansas 67208; (316) 689-3000.

Center for Innovation and Business Development, Box 8103, University Station, Grand Forks, North Dakota 58202; (701) 777-3132. (Provides low-cost invention evaluation and various types of assistance.)

Creative Education Foundation, Inc., 437 Franklin Street, Buffalo, New York 14202; (716) 884-2774.

Entrepreneurial Management Center, College of Business Administration, San Diego, California 92182; (619) 265-5306.

Entrepreneurship Program, School of Business Administration, Bridge Hall, Room 6, University of Southern California, University Park, Los Angeles, California 90089-1421; (213) 743-2089.

Entrepreneurship Center, College of Commerce, De Paul University, 25 East Jackson Blvd., Chicago, Illinois 60604; (312) 341-8471.

Florida Small Business Development Center System, State Coordinator, University of West Florida, Building 38, Pensacola, Florida 32514; (904) 474-3016. (Statewide program includes twenty centers. Write for list.)

Golden State Energy Center, Building 1055, Fort Cronkrite, Sausalito, California 94965; (415) 561-7692.

Innovation and Entrepreneurship Institute, School of Business, University of Miami, Post Office Box 249117, Coral Bavels, Florida 33124; (305) 284-4692.

Innovation Assessment Center, Small Business Development Center, College of Business and Economics, 441 Todd Hall, Washington State University, Pullman, Washington 99164-4740; (509) 335-5337 or 335-1576.

Invention Assessment Center, Washington State University, 180 Nickerson, Suite 310, Seattle, Washington 98109; (206) 464-5450.

Innovation Evaluation Program, Center for Entrepreneurship, James Madison University, Harrisonburg, Virginia 22807; (703) 568-6334. (Provides evaluations by industry experts for a nominal fee.)

International Association of Incubators, East Washington University, 216 Showalter Hall, Cheney, Washington 99004; (509) 359-2371.

Institute for Ventures in New Technology ("INVENT"), Suite 310, Energy Research Center, Texas A & M University, College Station, Texas 77843-3577; (409) 845-0538.

Resource Guide

Inventors Clubs of America, Post Office Box 450261, Atlanta, Georgia 30345; (404) 938-5089.

Inventors of California, Post Office Box 158, Rheem Valley, California 94570.

Inventors Workshop International Education Foundation, Post Office Box 251, Tarzana, California 91356; (818) 344-3375; toll-free: (800) 843-8443.

Karl Eller Center, College of Business and Public Administration, University of Arizona, Tucson, Arizona 85721; (602) 621-2125.

Licensing Executives Society ("LES"), Department LES, 20501 Ford Road, Dearborn, Michigan 48128; (313) 271-1500. (Publishes *Les Nouvelles*, a quarterly journal.)

Minnesota Inventors Congress, Inc., Post Office Box 71, Redwood Falls, Minnesota 56283-0071; (507) 637-2828. (Holds annual two-day convention and exhibition for display of inventions, second weekend in June.)

National Business Incubation Association, Post Office Box 882, Fairfax, Virginia 22030-0882; (717) 249-4508.

National Congress of Inventors Organizations, Post Office Box 158, Rheem Valley, California 94570; (415) 376-7541.

New Mexico Energy Research and Development Institute, Seed Capital Program for Entrepreneurial Energy Development, University of New Mexico, Room 358, Piñon Building, 1220 South St. Francis Drive, Santa Fe, New Mexico 87501; (505) 827-5886.

Office for Entrepreneurial Studies, College of Business Administration, University of Illinois, Box 4348, Chicago, Illinois 60680; (312) 996-2670.

Patent Office Society, Box 209, Arlington, Virginia 22202; (703) 557-2767. (Publishes a newsletter and journal.)

Rural Enterprises, Inc., Post Office Box 1335, Durant, Oklahoma 74701; (405) 924-5094.

Science and Technology Resource Center, Southwest State University, Marshall, Minnesota 56258; (507) 537-7440; toll-free: 1-800-642-0684 (Minnesota); 1-800-533-8605 (South Dakota, Iowa, North Dakota, Wisconsin, Nebraska). (Provides evaluations and business incubation.)

Society for the Encouragement of Research and Invention. Post Office Box 412, 100 Summit Avenue, Summit, New Jersey 07901.

Technology Idea Evaluation Program, Missouri Division of Community Economic Development, Post Office Box 118, Jefferson City, Missouri 65102.

Technical Innovation Program, Anderson School of Management, University of Arizona, 1920 Lomas N. E., Albuquerque, New Mexico 87131; (505) 277-6471.

Wharton Entrepreneurial Center, Wharton School, University of Pennsylvania, Suite 3200, Steinberg Hall-Detrick Hall, Philadelphia, Pennsylvania 19104; (215) 898-4856.

Wisconsin Innovation Service Center, University of Wisconsin Small Business Development Center, 402 McCutchan, University of Wisconsin, Whitewater, Wisconsin 53190-1790; (414) 472-1365. (Evaluates ideas for a small fee.)

GOVERNMENT RESOURCES

Agencies and Publications

Write the following agencies for information about their publications and services. Most publications can also be obtained from the Superintendent of Documents, Government Printing Office, Washington, D. C. 20402; (202) 783-3238.

Copyright Office, Library of Congress, Washington, D. C. 20559:
> *Circular R 1, Copyright Basics*
> *Circular R 15a, Duration of Copyright*
> *Circular R 34, Copyright Protection Not Available for Names, Titles, or Short Phrases*
> *Circular R 38a*
> *Circular R 99, Highlights of the New Copyright Law*
> *General Information Concerning Copyrights*

Defense Technical Information Center, Cameron Station, Alexandria, Virginia 22314.

Department of Commerce, Washington, D.C., 20234
> *Business Services Bulletins*
> *Publications Catalog and Index*
> *Distribution Data Guide*

Department of Energy, Assistant General Counsel for Patents, Washington, D. C. 20585.
> *You and the Patenting Process*
> *Small Business Guide to Federal R & D Funding Opportunities*

National Appropriate Technology Assistance Service, Department of Energy, POB 2525, Butte, Montana 59702-2525.

National Science Foundation, Small Business Innovation Research Program ("SBIR"), Room 1250, 1800 G Street N. W., Washington, D. C. 20550.

Resource Guide

National Science Foundation, Office of Small Business Research and
Development, Room 1121, 1800 G Street N. W., Washington, D. C.
20550; (202) 357-7527:
Selected Aspects of Consumer Behavior
Small Business Guide to Federal R & D Funding Opportunities

National Technical Information Service ("NTIS"), Center for the
Utilization of Federal Technology ("CUFT"), and Office of Federal
Patent Licensing, Department of Commerce, 5285 Port Royal Road,
Springfield, Virginia 22161; (703) 487-4600:
Abstract Newsletters, PR-205
Bibliographic Databases and other databases
Catalog of Government Patents, PR-735
Computer Software Directories, PR-572
Data Base Services and Federal Technology in Machine-Readable
Formats Catalog, PR-595
Directory of Computerized Data Files
Directory of Computer Software Available from NTIS, PR-261
Directory of Federal Technology Resources, PR-767
Energy Modeling Programs from the Energy Information
Administration, PR-705
Federal Energy Technology, PR-593
Federal Engineering Technology Catalog, PR-596
Federal Patent Licensing, PR-751
Federal Research in Progress ("FEDRIP") Database
Federal Software Center, PR-260
Federal Software Exchange Catalog, PR-383
Federal Technology Catalog, PR-732
Foreign Broadcast Information Service, PR-376
Foreign Technology Abstract Newsletter
Foreign Technology and Foreign Marketing Information Catalog,
PR-594
General Catalog of Information Services No. 9, PR-154
Government Inventions for Licensing, PR-750
Government Reports Announcements and Index ("GRA&I"), PR-195
Government Reports Annual Index, PR-273
NTIS Key Word Title Index to Bibliographic Data File, PR-567
Online Invention Brochure, PR-725
Patent and Trademark Products/Services, PR-694

Resource Guide

Public Use Data Tapes from the National Center for Health Statistics,
PR-716
Published Searches Master Catalog, PR-186
Published Searches Mini-Catalogs:
  Agriculture and Food, PR-670
  Business and Management, PR-667
  Communications and Electrotechnology, PR-666
  Computers, PR-673
  Energy, PR-668
  Engineering, PR-672
  Environment, PR-669
  Health and Medicine, PR-674
  Physical Sciences, PR-671
  A Reference Guide to the NTIS Bibliographic Data Base,
    PR-253
  SRIM Brochure, PR-270
  Statistical Data Files from the Energy Information
    Administration, PR-712
  Tech Notes Catalog, PR-365

Office of Energy-Related Inventions, National Bureau of Standards,
    Department of Commerce, Gaithersburg, Maryland 20899;
    (202) 921-1000:

Patent and Trademark Office, Washington, D. C. 20231; (703) 557-3158:
    Attorneys and Agents Registered to Practice Before the United
        States Patent and Trademark Office.
    Directory of Registered Patent Attorneys and Agents Arranged by
        States and Counties
    The Disclosure Document Program
    General Information Concerning Patents
    General Information Concerning Trademarks
    Guide for Patent Draftsmen
    Index of Patents Issued from the United States Patent and
    Trademark Office
    Index of Trademarks Issued from the United States Patent and
        Trademark Office
    Official Gazette of the United States Patent and Trademark Office
    Patent and Trademark Office Notices
    Patent Profiles

197

Resource Guide

Patents and Government Developed Inventions
Patents and Inventions: An Informal Aid for Inventors
Questions and Answers About Patents
Technology Assessment and Forecast
Trademark Rules of Practice with Forms and Statutes

Small Business Administration, Post Office Box 30, Denver, Colorado
80201-0030; toll-free: (800) 368-5855:
> *For Sale Management Assistance Publications (115B)* and *Free
> Management Assistance Publications (115A)*, listing
> currently available publications from SBA.
> *Monthly Products List Circular*
> Small Business Bibliographies
>> No. 9, *Marketing Research Procedures*
>> No. 12, *Statistics and Maps for National Market Analysis*
>> No. 13, *National Directories for Use in Marketing*
>> No. 18, *Basic Business Reference Sources*
>> No. 39, *Decision Points in Developing New Products*
>> No. 89, *Marketing for Small Business*
>> No. 90, *New Product Development*
>> No. 91, *Ideas into Dollars: A Resource Guide for Inventors
>> and Innovative Small Businesses*
> Small Business Innovation Research Programs, SBSA Office of
> Innovation Research and Technology, 1441 1 St. NW,
> Washington, D. C. 20416
> Management Aids:
>> No. 2.013, *Can You Make Money with Your Idea or
>> Invention?*
>> No. 4.019, *Learning About Your Market*
>> No. 2.006, *Finding a New Product for Your Company*
>> No. 6.005, *Introduction to Patents*

Superintendent of Documents, Government Printing Office, Washington,
D. C. 20402; (202) 783-3238. The publications of other
agencies are available from this agency.
> *Bureau of the Census Catalog*
> *Business Statistics*
> *Commerce Business Daily*
> *Directory of Federal Technology Transfe*
> *County and City Data Book*

Resource Guide

Guide for the Submission of Unsolicited Research and
Development Proposals
Guide to Invention and Innovation Evaluation
How to Keep in Touch with U.S. Government Publications
Measuring Markets: A Guide to the Use of Federal and State
Statistical Data
Monthly Catalog of United States Government Publications
Monthly Checklist of State Publications
New Books
Practical Business Use of Government Statistics
Price List 36, Government Periodicals and Subscription Services
Statistical Abstract of the United States
Subject Bibliography Index (SB-599)
Survey of Current Business
Trademark Official Gazette
U. S. Government Books: Publications for Sale by the United
States GPO.
U. S. Government Purchasing and Sales Directory

Small Business Development Centers

Bryant College
Smithfield, Rhode Island 02917
(401) 232-6000

Casper Community College
944 East Second Street
Casper, Wyoming 82601
(307) 235-4825

College of St. Thomas
1107 Hazeltine Gates Blvd.
Chaska, Minnesota 55318
448-8810

College of the Virgin Islands
Box 1087
Charlotte Amalie, St. Thomas 00801
(809) 776-3206

Department of Commerce
State of California
1121 L Street, Suite 600
Sacramento, California 95814
(916) 324-8102

Department of Commerce
  and Community Affairs
620 East Adams Street
Springfield, Illinois 62701
(217) 785-6174

Howard University
6th and Fairmount St. N. W.
Room 128
Washington, D. C. 20059
(202) 636-5150

Indiana Economic Dev. Council
1 North Capitol, Suite 200
Indianapolis, Indiana 46204
(317) 634-6407

Iowa State University
College of Business Admin.
205 Engineering Annex
Ames, Iowa 50011
(515) 294-3420

Lane Community College
Downtown Center
1059 Willamette Street
Eugene, Oregon 97401
(503) 726-2250 or 687-9144

Memphis State University
Fogelman College of Business
  and Economics
Memphis, Tennessee 38152
(901) 454-2500

Northeast Louisiana University
Administration 2-123
Monroe, Louisiana 71209
(318) 342-2464

Resource Guide

Ohio Dept. of Development
30 East Broad Street
Post Office Box 1001
Columbus, Ohio 43266-1001
(614) 466-4945

St. Louis University
3642 Lindell Blvd.
St. Louis, Missouri 63108
(314) 534-7232

State University of New York
State University Plaza
Albany, New York 12246
(518) 473-5398

University of Arkansas
New Business Building
33d and University Avenue
Little Rock, Arkansas 72204
(501) 371-5381

University of Connecticut
Box U-41, Room 422
368 Fairfield Road
Storrs, Connecticut 06268
(203) 486-4135

University of Georgia
Chicopee Complex
Athens, Georgia 30602
(404) 542-5760

University of Kentucky
18 Porter Building
Lexington, Kentucky 40506-0205
(606) 257-1751

Rutgers University
Ackerson Hall - 3d Floor
180 University Street
Newark, New Jersey 07102
(201) 648-5950

Southeastern Oklahoma State Univ.
Station A, Box 4194
Durant, Oklahoma 74701
(405) 924-0277

University of Alabama School of Business
1717 11th Avenue S., Suite 419
Birmingham, Alabama 35294
(205) 934-7260

University of Charleston
2300 MacCorkle Avenue S. E.
Charleston, West Virginia 25304
(304) 357-4800

University of Delaware
Suite 005 - Purnell Hall
Newark, Delaware 19711
(302) 451-2747

University of Houston
University Park
127 Heyne
4800 Calhoun
Houston, Texas 77004
(713) 749-4236

University of Massachusetts
School of Management
Amherst, Massachusetts 01003
(413) 549-4930

Resource Guide

University of Mississippi
3825 Ridgewood Road
Jackson, Mississippi 39211
(601) 982-6760

University of Nebraska
Peter Kiewit Center
Omaha, Nebraska 68182
(402) 554-2521

University of Nevada
College of Business Admin.
Reno, Nevada 89557-0016
(702) 784-1717

University of New Hampshire
McConnell Hall
Durham, New Hampshire 03824
(603) 862-3558

University of North Carolina
820 Clay Street
Raleigh, North Carolina
(919) 733-4643

University of North Dakota
College of Business & Public Admin
Grand Forks, North Dakota 58202
(701) 777-2224

University of Pennsylvania
The Wharton School
3201 Steinberg Hall -
  Deitrich Hall/CC
Philadelphia, Pennsylvania 19104

University of Puerto Rico
College Station
Building B
Mayaguez, Puerto Rico 00708
(809) 834-3590 or 834-3790

University of South Carolina
College of Business Administration
Columbia, South Carolina 29208
(803) 777-4907

University of South Dakota
Business Research Bureau
School of Business
Vermillion, South Dakota 57069
(605) 677-5272

University of Southern Maine
246 Deering Avenue
Portland, Maine 04102
(207) 780-4423

University of Texas
College of Engineering
Post Office Box 19209
Arlington, Texas 76019
(817) 273-2559

University of Utah
420 Chipeta Way, Suite 110
Salt Lake City, Utah 84108
(801) 581-4869

University of Vermont
Extension Service
Morrill Hall
Burlington, Vermont 05405
(802) 656-4479

Resource Guide

University of West Florida
Building 38, Room 107
Pensacola, Florida 32514-5752
(904) 474-3016

Washington State University
College of Business & Economics
Pullman, Washington 99164
(509) 335-1576

Wichita State University
College of Business Administration
1845 Fairmount
Wichita, Kansas 67208
(316) 689-3193

University of Wisconsin
609 State Street, 2d Floor
Madison, Wisconsin 53703
(608) 263-7794

Wayne State University
Metropolitan Center for
  High Technology
Detroit, Michigan 48201
(313) 577-4848

Federal Patent Depository Libraries

Alabama	Auburn University Libraries
	Birmingham Public Library
Arizona	Tempe: Science Library, Arizona State University
California	Los Angeles Public Library
	Sacramento: California State Library
	San Diego Public Library
	Sunnyvale: Patent Information Clearinghouse
Colorado	Denver Public Library
Delaware	Newark: University of Delaware
Georgia	Atlanta: Price Gilbert Memorial Library, Georgia Institute of Technology
Idaho	Moscow: University of Idaho Library
Illinois	Chicago Public Library
	Springfield: Illinois State Library
Indiana	Indianapolis: Marion County Public Library
Louisiana	Baton Rouge: Troy H. Middleton Library, Lousiana State University
Maryland Sciences	College Park: Engineering and Physical Library, University of Maryland
Massachusetts	Boston Public Library
Michigan	Ann Arbor: Engineering Transportation Library, University of Michigan
	Detroit Public Library
Minnesota	Minneapolis Public Library and Information Center
Missouri	Kansas City: Linda Hall Library
	St. Louis Public Library
Montana	Butte: Montana College of Mineral Science and Technology
Nebraska	Lincoln: University of Nebraska-Lincoln, Engineering Library
Nevada	Reno: University of Nevada Library
New Hampshire	Durham: University of Nevada Library
New Jersey	Newark Public Library
New Mexico	Albuquerque: University of New Mexico Library

New York	Albany: New York State Library
	Buffalo and Erie County Library
	New York Public Library (The Research
	Libraries)
North Carolina	Raleigh: D. H. Hill Library, North Carolina
	State University
Ohio	Public Library of Cincinnati and Hamilton
	County
	Cleveland Public Library
	Columbus: Ohio State University
	Libraries
	Toledo/Lucas County Public Library
Oklahoma	Stillwater: Oklahoma State University
	Library
Pennsylvania	Cambridge Springs: Alliance College
	Library
	Philadelphia: Franklin Institute Library
	Pittsburgh: Carnegie Library of
	Pittsburgh
	University Park: Pattee Library,
Pennsylvania	State University
Rhode Island	Providence Public Library
South Carolina	Charleston: Medical University of South
	Carolina
Tennessee	Memphis and Shelby County Public Library
	and Information Center
Texas	Austin: McKinney Engineering Library,
	University of Texas
	College Station: Sterling C. Evans Library,
	Texas A & M University
	Dallas Public Library
	Houston: The Fondren Library, Rice
	University
Utah	Salt Lake City: Marriott Library University
	of Utah
Washington	Seattle: Engineering Library, University of
	Washington
Wisconsin	Madison: Kurt F. Wendt Engineering
	Library, University of Wisconsin
	Milwaukee Public Library

SAMPLE FORMS

CONFIDENTIALITY AGREEMENT

We agree to receive in confidence full details about an idea or invention to be submitted by [your name].

In consideration for receiving such information, we agree that all materials provided shall remain the property of [your name] and that they will be returned immediately upon written request.

We agree to maintain the confidentiality of all information and materials provided and to refrain from divulging any details of the idea or invention without prior written consent.

We agree not to make use of any feature or information of which [your name] is the originator, without payment of compensation in an amount to be negotiated.

The idea or invention is being received and will be reviewed in confidence. However, we assume no responsibility whatsoever with respect to features or related technology that can be demonstrated to be already known to us. All information and correspondence regarding the subject of this agreement shall be marked "CONFIDENTIAL."

We agree that within a period of __ days we will report to [your name] the results of our review and will advise whether we are interested in negotiating for the purchase of the rights to use the idea or invention.

Date: _____   Company:_____

By:_____
Title:_____

IDEA SUBMISSION AGREEMENT AND WAIVER
OF CONFIDENTIALITY

Name of invention or idea: _____.
Submitted by: _____.

I am submitting with this agreement a description of an invention or idea that I believe to be unique and novel in order to determine whether _____ ("the Company") would be interested in acquiring any or all of my rights under common law or statutory law, including patent, copyright, trademark, and other rights.

This submission is made voluntarily. I understand that the Company may have prior knowledge of or may have developed or be developing a similar invention or idea. In consideration of the Company reviewing my idea or invention, I agree that the following terms apply to this submission:

A.   This submission does not create or imply a confidential relationship;

B.   This submission does not impose any obligation, express or implied, for compensation or otherwise, except as may later be provided in a written agreement between me and the Company.

C.   The Company assumes no obligation to consider or evaluate my submission or to do any more at any time than to give me its decision as to its interest in pursuing it. The Company has no obligation to give me any information about its activities in the field related to my invention or idea or to give me any reasons for its decisions. The Company's evaluation of my submission shall not be construed as a recognition of its originality or novelty.

D.   This submission does not impair or affect in any way the Company's right to contest my patent, trademark, copyright, or other proprietary interests in my idea or invention.

E. I represent that, to the best of my knowledge and belief, I am the sole inventor or originator and owner of the submitted idea or invention.

F. No license or right whatsoever is granted by this submission agreement. The Company incurs no obligation to me of any kind for use of my idea or invention unless and until a formal agreement is executed between us. In the absence of such an agreement, my rights shall be limited to those existing under the patent, trademark, and copyright laws.

G. The Company assumes no obligation to return any of the materials I have submitted and no responsibility for their damage or loss.

H. Enclosed with this submission are the following documents, of which I have kept copies [check as appropriate]:

____ Written statement dated _____ explaining the idea or invention;
____ Plans, photographs, description of the idea or invention;
____ Copy of registered trademark no. _____;
____ Copy of trademark application on file in the United States Patent and Trademark Office;
____ Copy of copyright registration on file with the Library of Congress;
____ Copy of patent no. _____;
____ Copy of patent application on file in the United States Patent and Trademark Office.

Date:_____.

Signature:_____.

NONEXCLUSIVE LICENSING AGREEMENT

This agreement is made between _____ ("licensor") and _____ ("licensee") on _____, 19____.

Licensor is the sole inventor and owner of _____ _____("the product") and certain information, technical data, processes, know-how, shop practices, drawings, plans, specifications, methods of manufacture, and other data relating to the product ("the information"). Licensee desires to obtain a nonexclusive license to utilize the information and to manufacture and sell the product. In consideration of the mutual promises in this agreement, the parties agree as follows:

1. Scope. This agreement shall be limited to the product and the information.

2. License. Subject to the terms of this agreement, licensor grants to licensee the nonexclusive, nontransferable right and license to use the information to manufacture the product and to sell or lease the product throughout the world. No license, express or implied, is granted to employ the information for any other purpose whatsoever.

3. Compensation.
　　　　a. Advance against royalties. Within ___ days of executing this agreement, licensee shall pay licensor a nonrefundable advance against royalties in the amount of $_____. Royalties actually accrued shall be applied against this advance. If royalties do not equal the amount of the advance, licensor shall not be required to reimburse licensee.
　　　　b. Royalties. Licensee shall pay licensor a royalty of ____ percent of the gross sales or lease price collected by licensee on each product sold or leased, subject to an annual minimum royalty of $_____ per calendar year, prorated for the first year in which commercial distribution began. Payment of royalties shall be made for ___ years, beginning with the date of the first sale of the product by the licensee.

c. Records. Licensee shall maintain accurate records relating to the manufacture and sale of the product. Licensee shall render quarterly reports to licensor within three weeks of the end of each quarter showing the total quantity of the product produced; the quantity sold, leased, or otherwise utilized; the gross receipts received by licensor for such transactions; and the amounts due licensor as royalties. Licensor or an authorized representative shall have the right to inspect and copy such records and books of account upon licensor's written request, and such inspection and copying shall be done during licensee's regular business hours. All books of account and records shall be kept available for licensee's inspection for at least two years after the termination of this agreement.

d. Payment. Royalties for the preceding quarter shall be paid to licensor with each quarterly report.

4. Licensee agrees to exert reasonable, diligent efforts to manufacture and promote the sale of the product as soon as possible, but no later than _____, 19___, and to satisfy the demand for the product. Licensee agrees that the product shall bear its name, exclusive of all others.

5. Until _____, 19___, licensor will provide licensee with information, as available, relating to improvements and changes in the product. Upon written request from licensee, licensor will provide further detailed information to the extent available in order to determine whether the improvements and changes may be of use to licensor. Upon receipt of an invoice from licensor, licensee shall, with the next scheduled payment, reimburse licensor for all reasonable costs and expense incurred in fulfilling these obligations. Improvements and related addititonal items conceived of or created by licensor shall be the basis for renegotiation of the royalty terms of this agreement.

6. Consultant services. The services of licensor as consultant shall be available to licensee on a part-time basis at the rate of $_____ per hour, plus expenses.

7. Termination of the agreement.
    a. Unless terminated sooner, this agreement shall remain in force through _____, 19___.
    b. Either party shall have the right to terminate this contract if the other party fails to perform as agreed, provided that such failure shall not have been remedied by the defaulting party within sixty days of having received written notice of intention to terminate.
    c. Bankruptcy or insolvency of licensee shall automatically terminate this agreement.
    d. Any assignment or attempted assignment by licensee shall automatically terminate this agreement.
    e. Licensee shall have the right to sell or lease any products on hand or contracted for as of the date of termination. Any termination shall not release licensee from payment of royalties accrued through the date of termination.

8. Waiver of any breach of this agreement shall not be deemed a waiver of any subsequent breach.

9. This agreement shall be interpreted in accordance with the laws of the State of _____.

10. Licensee agrees to make adequate warnings for the product, comply with all applicable laws and regulations, and carry third-party liability insurance to insure and adequately cover both licensor and licensee against claims resulting from damage or personal injury through sale or use of the product. Licensee agrees to name licensor as an additional insured on all such insurance policies.

11. No terms of this agreement can be waived or modified except by an express agreement in writing signed by both parties. There are no representations, promises, warranties, or covenants other than those contained in this document. This represents the entire agreement of the parties.

12. The provisions of this agreement are severable. If any provision of this agreement is held to be invalid or unenforceable, the rest shall continue in full force and effect.

13. Any notice, payment, or report required or allowed under this agreement shall be deemed given when sent by registered mail to the other party at its address of record. The record addresses of the parties may be changed by written notice.

Licensor:_____.

Licensee:_____.

Executed this __ day of _____, 19__, at _____.

SELECTED BIBLIOGRAPHY

Adams, James L. *Conceptual Blockbusting: A Guide to Better Ideas.* 2d ed. New York: Norton, 1980.

Andreasen, Alan R. "Cost-Conscious Marketing Research." *Harvard Business Review* 61, no. 4 (July-August 1983) 74-79.

Barnes, Carl E. "Get Inventions Off the Shelf." *Harvard Business Review* 44, no. 1 (January-February 1966) 138-39.

Berg, Thomas L. *Mismarketing: Case Histories of Marketing Misfires.* New York: Doubleday, 1970.

Brabham, Vernon, Jr. *How to Turn Your Ideas into Big Money.* Marietta, Georgia: Craftmark, 1982.

Britt, Steuart H., ed. *The Spenders.* McGraw-Hill Series in Marketing and Advertising. New York: McGraw-Hill, 1960.

Britt, Steuart Henderson, and Irwin A. Shapiro. "How to Find Marketing Facts." *Harvard Business Review* 40, no. 5 (September-October 1962) 44-50, 171-78.

Brosnahan, Carol S., ed. *Attorney's Guide to Trade Secrets.* Berkeley, California: California Continuing Education of the Bar, 1971 [supplement 1983 by Louis J. Knobbe.]

Brown, Frederick, and Joann Swanson. "Maintaining the Competitive Edge—Lawful Protection of Trade Secrets." *Employee Relations Law Journal* 10, no. 3 (Winter 1984-85). 374-99.

Brown, Lawrence A. *Innovation Diffusion: A New Perspective.* New York: Methuen, 1981.

Bruner, Jerome. *On Knowing: Essays for the Left Hand.* Cambridge, Mass.: Harvard University Press, 1966.

Buggie, Frederick D. *New Product Development Strategies.* New York: AMACOM, 1981.

___. "Focus Groups: Searching for the 'Right' Product." *Management Review* 72, no. 4 (April 1983) 39-41.

Campbell, Hannah. *Why Did They Name It . . . ?* New York: Fleet, 1964.

Clark, Charles H. *Idea Management: How to Motivate Creativity and Innovation.* New York: AMACOM, 1980.

Crawford, Robert P. *Techniques of Creative Thinking.* New York: Hawthorn, 1954.

Selected Bibliography

Crawford, C. Merle. *New Products Management.* Homewood, Illinois: Irwin, 1983.

Davis, Gary A. *Psychology of Problem Solving: Theory and Practice.* New York: Basic Books, 1973.

De Bono, Edward. *New Think: The Use of Lateral Thinking in the Generation of New Ideas.* New York: Basic Books, 1968.

_____. *Eureka! An Illustrated History of Inventions from the Wheel to the Computer.* New York: Holt, Rinehart & Winston, 1974 *Marketing News* 14, no. 7 (October 3, 1980).

Dunlavy, Dean C. "Protection of the Inventor Outside the Patent System." *California Law Review* 43; 1955, 457-76.

Edwards, Betty. *Drawing on the Right Side of the Brain.* Los Angeles: Tarcher, 1979.

Engel, James F., and Roger D. Blackwell. *Consumer Behavior.* Chicago: Dryden Press, 1982.

Ferber, Robert. *Handbook of Marketing Research.* New York: McGraw-Hill, 1974.

Finkin, Eugene F. "Developing and Managing New Products." *Journal of Business Strategy* 3, no. 4 (Spring 1983) 39-46.

Forman, Howard I. "Problems Involved in the Protection, Buying, and Selling of Inventions." *Journal of the Patent Office Society* 41 (August 1959) 531-61.

Foxall, Gordon R. *Consumer Behavior: A Practical Guide.* New York: Halsted/Wiley, 1980.

Frech, E. Bryant. "Scorecard for New Products: How to Pick a Winner." *Management Review* 66, no. 2 (February 1977) 4-11.

Gordon, William J. J. *Synectics: The Development of Creative Capacity.* New York: Harper & Row, 1961.

Goydon, Raymond. "Phantom Products." *Forbes* 133 (May 21, 1984) 202.

Gryskievicz, Stanley S., ed. *Proceedings of Creativity Week* Series. Greensboro, N. C.: Center for Creative Leadership, 1979-84.

Gumpert, David E., and Jeffry A. Timmons. *The Insider's Guide to Small Business Resources.* Garden City, New York: Doubleday, 1982.

Haefele, John W. *Creativity and Innovation.* New York: Reinhold, 1962.

Hall, Woody. *Your Ideas May Be Worth a Fortune.* Lake San Marcos, California, 1979.

Hanan, Mack. *Life-Styled Marketing.* Rev. ed. New York: AMACOM, 1980.

Selected Bibliography

Hartley, Robert F. *Marketing Mistakes.* 2d ed. Columbus, Ohio: Grid, 1981.

Hawkins, Del I., and Gerald G. Udell. "Corporate Caution and Unsolicited New Product Ideas: A Survey of Corporate Waiver Requirements." *Journal of the Patent Office Society* 58, no. 6 (June 1976) 375-88.

Heany, Donald F. "Degrees of Product Innovation." *Journal of Business Strategy* 3, no. 4 (Spring 1983) 3-14

Holtz, Herman R. *Profit from Your Money-Making Ideas: How to Build a New Business or Expand an Existing One.* New York: AMACOM, 1980.

"How to Keep Well-Intentioned Research from Misleading New Product Planners." *Marketing News* 18, no. 1 (January 6, 1984) sec. 2 p. 1.

Jewkes, John, David Sawyers, and Richard Stillerman. *The Sources of Invention.* 2d ed. New York: Norton, 1969.

Klompmaker, Jay E., G. David Hughes, and Russell I. Haley. "Test Marketing in New Product Development." *Harvard Business Review* 54, no. 3 (May-June 1976) 128-38.

Koberg, Don, and Jim Bagnall. *Universal Traveler: A Soft-Systems Guide to Creativity, Problem-Solving, and the Process of Reaching Goals.* 4th ed. Los Altos, California: Kaufmann, 1981.

Koestler, Arthur. *The Act of Creation.* London: Hutchinson, 1976.

Kracke, Don, with Roger Honkanen. *How to Turn Your Idea into a Million Dollars.* New York: Mentor/New American Library, 1977.

Landis, Stephen P. "Marketing Researchers: Screen New Product Ideas, Ad Claims with Need-Gap Rating System." *Marketing News* 17 (May 13, 1983) sec. 2, p. 13.

Langer, Judith. "Consumer Research: Critical Step in New Product Development." *Marketing Times* 30, no. 2 (April 19, 1983) 28-32.

Lee, Donald D. *Industrial Marketing Research: Techniques and Practices.* 2d ed. New York: Van Nostrand Reinhold, 1984.

Luck, David, J., et al. *Marketing Research.* 6th ed. Englewood Cliffs: Prentice-Hall, 1978.

McKim, Robert H. *Experiences in Visual Thinking.* 2d ed. Monterey, California: Brooks/Cole, 1980.

MacKinnon, Donald W. *In Search of Human Effectiveness: Identifying and Developing Creativity.* Buffalo, New York: Creative Education Foundation, 1978.

McTavish, Ronald. "Company Practice in New Product Evaluation." *Journal of General Management* 8, no. 1 (Autumn 1982) 69-82.

215

Selected Bibliography

Maidique, Modesto A. "Entrepreneurs, Champions, and Technical Innovation." *Sloan Management Review* 21, no. 2 (Winter 1980) 59-76.

Main, Jeremy. "Help and Hype in the New-Products Game." *Fortune* 107, no. 3 (February 7, 1983) 60-64.

Management of the New Product Function: A Guidebook. New York: Association of National Advertisers, 1980.

Marting, Elizabeth, ed. *New Products/New Profits: Company Experiences in New Product Planning.* New York: American Management Association, 1964.

Michman, Ronald D. "New Directions for Lifestyle Behavior Patterns." *Business Horizons* 27, no. 4 (July-August 1984) 59-64.

Morley, John, ed. *Launching a New Product.* London: Businesss Books, 1968.

Moskowitz, Milton, Michael Katz, and Robert Levering, eds. *Everybody's Business: An Almanac: The Irreverent Guide to Corporate America.* San Francisco: Harper and Row, 1980.

"New Product Programs Hinge on Right People, Many Ideas, Evaluation System." *Marketing News* 17, no. 18 (September 2, 1983) 10.

Osborn, Alex F. *Applied Imagination: Principles and Procedures of Creative Problem-Solving.* 3d rev. ed. New York: Scribner, 1963.

Paige, Richard E. *Complete Guide to Making Money with Your Ideas and Inventions.* Tarzana, California: ILMA, 1983.

Papanek, Victor. *Design for the Real World: Human Ecology and Social Change.* 2d ed. New York: Van Nostrand Reinhold, 1984.

Parker, Henrik D. "Reform for Rights of Employed Inventors." *Southern California Law Revew* 57, no. 4 (May 1984) 603-29.

Parnes, Sidney Jay, and Harold F. Harding, eds. *A Source Book for Creative Thinking.* New York: Scribner 1962.

Perkins, D. N. *The Mind's Best Work.* Cambridge, Massachusetts: Harvard University Press, 1981.

Pinchot, Gifford, III. *Intrapreneuring: Why You Don't Have to Leave the Corporation to Become an Entrepreneur.* New York: Harper & Row, 1985.

Pooley, James. *Trade Secrets: How to Protect Your Ideas and Assets.* Berkeley, California: Osborne/McGraw-Hill, 1982.

Prince, George M. *The Practice of Creativity: A Manual for Dynamic Group Problem Solving.* New York: Macmillan, 1972.

Selected Bibliography

Quinn, James Brian. "Technological Innovation, Entrepreneurship, and Strategy." *Sloan Management Review* 20, no. 3 (Spring 1979) 19-30.

Reefman, Walter E. *How to Sell Your Own Invention.* North Hollywood, California: Halls of Ivy Press, 1977.

Reynolds, Fred D., and William D. Wells. *Consumer Behavior.* New York: McGraw Hill, 1977.

Reynolds, William H. *Products and Markets.* New York: Appleton-Century-Crofts/Meredith, 1969.

Rico, Gabriele Lusser. *Writing the Natural Way.* Los Angeles: Tarcher, 1983.

Ries, Al, and Jack Trout. *Positioning: The Battle for Your Mind.* New York. McGraw-Hill, 1980.

Robson, Britt. "Intrapreneurship: Making Those Inside Moves." *Black Enterprise* (June 1985) 197.

Rogers, Everett M. *Diffusion of Innovations.* 3d ed. New York: The Free Press, 1983.

Rohan, Thomas M. "Are 'Ornery' Innovators Best? Experts Differ on Product-Development Teams." *Industry Week* 217, no. 5 (May 30, 1983) 23-26.

Rosenau, Milton D., Jr. *Innovation: Managing the Development of Profitable New Products.* Engineering Series. Belmont, California: Lifetime Learning Publ., 1982.

Rosenbloom, Bert. *Retail Marketing.* New York, Random House: 1981.

Rothberg, Robert R., ed. *Corporate Strategy and Product Innovation.* 2d ed. New York: Free Press, 1981.

Schollhammer, Hans, and Arthur H. Kuriloff. *Entrepreneurship and Small Business Management.* New York: John Wiley, 1979.

Shook, Robert L. *Why Didn't I Think of That!* New York: New American Library, 1982.

Siposs, George G. *How to Cash in on Your Bright Ideas!* Orange, California: Universal Developments, 1980.

Spanner, Robert A. *Who Owns Innovation: The Rights and Obligations of Employers and Employees.* Homewood, Illinois: Dow Jones-Irvin, 1984.

Springer, Sally P., and Georg Deutsch. *Left Brain, Right Brain.* Rev. ed. New York: Freeman, 1985.

Stanton, William J. *Fundamentals of Marketing.* 5th ed. New York: McGraw-Hill, 1978.

Selected Bibliography

Stumpe, Warren R. " Right Entrepreneurial Stuff." *Les Nouvelles, Journal of the Licensing Executives Society* 20, no. 1 (March 1985) 17-19.

Submitting an Idea. American Bar Association, Section of Patent, Trademark and Copyright Law, 1974.

Tauber, Edward M. "Marketing Notes and Communications: Reduce New Product Failures: Measure Needs as Well as Purchase Interest." *Journal of Marketing* 37 (July 1973) 61-64.

___. "How Market Research Discourages Major Innovation." *Business Horizons* 17, no. 3 (June 1974) 22-26.

Tierney, Christine. "Intrapreneuring Employees Provide Companies Homegrown Entrepreneurs." *Washington Business Journal* (March 18, 1985) 1.

Todd, Alden. *Finding Facts Fast: How to Find Out What You Want and Need to Know.* 2d ed. Berkeley, California: Ten Speed Press, 1979.

Udell, Gerald G. "The Essential Nature of the Idea Brokerage Function." *Journal of the Patent Office Society* 57, no. 10 (October 1975) 642-58.

Udell, Gerald G., Kenneth O. Baker, and Gerald S. Albalm. "Creativity: Necessary But Not Sufficient." *Journal of Creative Behavior* 10, no. 2 (2d quarter 1976) 92-103.

Udell, Gerald G., and Michael F. O'Neill. "Technology Transfer: Encouraging the Noncorporate Inventor." *Business Horizons* 20, no. 4 (August 1977) 40-45.

Von Hipple, Eric A. "Get New Products from Customers." *Harvard Business Review* 60 (March/April 1982) 117.

___. "Has a Customer Already Developed Your Next Product?" *Sloan Management Review,* 18, no. 2 (Winter 1977) 63-74.

Wind, Yoram, Vijay Mahajan, and Richard N. Cardozo, eds. *New Product Forecasting: Models and Applications.* Lexington, Massachusetts: Lexington Books/Heath, 1981.

Witt, Scott. *How to be Twice as Smart: Boosting Your Brainpower and Unleashing the Miracles of Your Mind.* West Nyack, New York: Parker, 1983.

Zimmer, David J. "Consider the Users' Real Needs When You Develop New Products." *Industrial Research* 25 (October 1983) 148.

Zotti, Ed. "Ideas Brew in Inventors' Kitchens." *Advertising Age* 53 (July 12, 1982) M10.

INDEX

K

WE WANT TO HEAR FROM YOU

To:
Ten Speed Press
P.O. Box 7123
Berkeley, California 94707

I would like to see the following changes, additions, or updates in the next edition of *THAT'S A GREAT IDEA!*

_____

_____

_____

_____

_____

_____

_____

_____

_____

Mail Order Moonlighting
by Cecil C. Hoge, Sr.

One of the most successful mail order books published now apppears in its first completely revised and updated edition. It has the unique perspective that mail order is best started small and can easily be done from home, literally on the kitchen table. "The authoritative and best up-to-date word for anyone in the mail order business or planning to start one."—*The Next Whole Earth Catalog*

6×9 inches   416 pages $9.95 paper

What Color Is Your Parachute?
by Richard N. Bolles

Based upon the latest research, this new, completely revised and updated edition is designed to give the most practical step-by-step help imaginable to the career-changer or job-hunter, whether he or she is sixteen or sixty-five. Questions asked throughout the cross-country research upon which this book is based, were: What methods of job-hunting and career-changing work best? What new methods have been developed by the best minds in this field? Is it possible to change jobs without going back for lengthy retraining?

6×9 inches   384 pages $8.95 paper $15.95 cloth

How to Be an Importer and Pay for Your World Travel
by Mary Green & Stanley Gillmar

The standard reference for the small do-it-yourself importer. It tells where to go to find products, what to buy, how to pay for it, and how to get it home and sell it for a profit. "An excellent, readable, complete and wise book."—*Whole Earth Catalog*

5½×8½ inches   192 pages $6.95 paper

What the World Needs Now
by Stephen M. Johnson

"One of the funniest and most ingenious titles in the field. There is just no limit to the range of practical weirdness covered."—*Patricia Holt, San Francisco Chronicle*

7¾×9¼ inches   160 pages $7.95 paper

Mail Order Know-How
by Cecil C. Hoge, Sr.

"*Mail Order Know-How*, suggests Hoge, can be gained by osmosis, by immersion in the world of direct marketing. With this volume he offers such immersion, through 125 short chapters that include experiences, advice, and strategies gleaned from his own knowledge and from interviews with other experts in the field. Like Hoge's *Mail Order Moonlighting* it is packed with information that is difficult to get at in an orderly fashion."—*Library Journal*

8½×11 inches   472 pages $16.95 paper $19.95 cloth